Living in
Daylight

Maria-Therese Hoppe

Living in Daylight

VELUX influence
on European living

Gyldendal

Contents

7   Foreword

9   Living in daylight, introduction
27   Changing the home
95   Choosing the home
133   Lighting up the city loft
183   Working under the roof
225   Preserving historic heritage
281   Creating future visions for daylight

Villum Kann Rasmussen with his children Aino and Lars in spring 1942. Despite the heavy workload associated with starting the company, there was also time to relax.

Foreword

In Copenhagen in late 1941, my father, Villum Kann Rasmussen, at that time a young graduate engineer, had just started his own construction company which specialised in glazing. Business was bad, as an ice-cold wartime winter held the country in its grip, and my father was in desperate need of customers. Around Christmas time, he was approached by an architect who asked for his help in constructing a skylight to be used in the sloped roof of a series of primary school projects on the Danish island of Zealand.

Back in those days, my father's business was a one-man-show but he took up the challenge and developed his vision for the project: 'Once and for all to make a skylight – a roof window – that in every respect is just as good as the best vertical window'.

This was the beginning of an industrial adventure. VELUX roof windows, as he named his 'child', would become the most well-known and respected brand world-wide within the field of building components. Today, millions of people in Europe and elsewhere enjoy daylight, fresh air and outlook through their roof windows and skylights every day as a result of his vision.

It is not possible to imagine contemporary living, the culture of homes and the architecture today without VELUX. This book, Living in Daylight, is all about how VELUX changed European living.

Lars E. Kann-Rasmussen

Living in
daylight,
introduction

Living in daylight, introduction

Living in daylight is a journey that visits homes, workplaces and heritage buildings in the amazing variety of European countries. The journey is organised in seven themes:

Empowering the customer lays the foundation for the journey by looking at the relationship between VELUX and its customers over time and how the vision of the company's founder foresaw the importance of new consumer expectations and dreams.

Changing the home is about people who have changed an old house into a contemporary, light-filled framework for their daily life. They live in houses built in different styles at various times in the cities of Amsterdam, Aarhus and Tallin, in suburbs of Paris and Copenhagen, in small towns in Brittany and England, and in villages in Switzerland, Portugal and Germany.

Choosing the home visits people living in new, imaginative homes, all permeated by daylight and opening up to the outdoors. We visit new houses with spectacular views of the landscape off the rocky Norwegian coast, in a tiny mountain village in the Spanish Pyrenees, and on the southern coast of Sweden, as well as exclusive, gated communities in the growing megacities of Moscow and Istanbul, an open child-friendly estate affordable for first-time buyers in the densely populated Netherlands, and finally innovatively designed apartments chosen by new seniors in the Netherlands.

Lighting up the city loft visits former lofts in the centres of European cities, a lifestyle setting regarded today as the height of attractiveness. One family has converted a loft in a protected historic area in the Castle Hill district of Budapest; another has transformed undesirable features from the past into a contemporary living unit in a former bomb shelter in Cologne. Others again have changed nondescript loft areas in Copenhagen and Milan into spacious, contemporary homes, while developers in Vienna have created better insulation and eco-friendly solutions in former slum houses. In St. Petersburg, a completely new penthouse floor was added to the flat roof of a concrete high-rise. An artist enjoys her view over the roofs of Paris; in Madrid and Sofia, two young architect couples – quite independently of each other – have converted old artists' studios into bright, open spaces.

Working under the roof looks at how new contemporary workplaces have been created under old roofs: the IT department of the Portuguese Parliament in Lisbon, a restored shopping area in Berlin, a former car-repair shop in Copenhagen changed into a concert hall, a disused Swiss railway storehouse into a high school, a former hayloft into a hothouse for growing cocoa trees in Denmark, a war-ravaged house in Sarajevo with hope for the future, a military gunpowder depot in Norway turned into a webshop, and a giant pigeon-infested loft in Gdańsk into workplaces for students at the university.

Preserving historic heritage looks at the way changes are enabling old, even ancient buildings and structures to function in a modern context while preserving the heritage. In Russia we see the shining Peter-Paul fortress in St. Petersburg, in Paris three palace complexes in the heart of the city, in Copenhagen a former hippie squat among historic moats and defence works. We visit medieval castles in France and Belgium and look at changes that preserve modest Victorian workers' terraced houses in England,

an aristocratic villa in the Czech Republic, a shooting gallery in Hungary and a captain's house in Brittany.

And finally, **Creating future visions for daylight** presents ways in which VELUX is continuing the tradition of its founder by developing new concepts and products enabling future customers to realise their new dreams of sustainability, of a better indoor climate – and of even more daylight.

Looking at Europe from above

European buildings have an amazing variety of styles. Even within a single country, charmingly different regional characteristics can still be found. This variety and beauty is one of the joys of travelling through the countries of Europe. Panoramic views of landscapes and cityscapes are favourite sights on any tourist itinerary. Looking down from above, we can admire the many different 'bella vistas', 'belle vues' and 'must-see' sights of the cities, with the focus on church spires and gables, imposing palaces, monuments, the towering roofs of ancient buildings in a rich variety of styles, the intricate patterns of streets that may be centuries or even millennia old, or the cosy quaintness of small towns.

But one aspect is rarely noticed, perhaps because it is so self-evident, so unprepossessing, so 'just there': the roofscapes with VELUX roof windows. In any town, any city, anywhere in the countryside, you will find them. It is only when you look at old photos that you notice the difference: in former times buildings had very few, very small skylights. When European children of today are asked to draw a house, they inevitably draw one with a sloping roof and one or more roof windows. With children in other parts of the world, this is generally not the case.

Quietly, almost imperceptibly, the roof windows have changed the look of European buildings, and – perhaps even more importantly – the way Europeans live in them.

Empowering the customer

In the years after the Second World War, Europe experienced a baby boom, when the largest generation ever of European children was born. Living conditions were not easy for young families in the post-war period: the housing shortage was severe, maintenance was inadequate and there was also a shortage of construction materials. Schools had been damaged by other uses during the war, and those still in use were bursting at the seams with the many new pupils continuously pouring in.

These young Europeans wanted to make their children their first priority. Traditionally, children did not have 'a room of their own' in the family home, as is evident from the plans of older houses: there is no sign of any 'children's room' anywhere. But the new generation of parents wanted things to be different: no more bundling their kids into anonymous corners in small, pokey apartments and houses. They wanted room, space and light for their children.

Many family homes contained space that no one had thought about before as suitable living space: attics and lofts. The children of former generations in the countryside had sometimes slept in these dark, unheated, draughty spaces under the roofs, as had many maids and other servants. But this was unthinkable for the new generation: their children deserved the best!

The loft, from ugly duckling to beautiful swan
The creation of the VELUX idea by Mr Villum Kann Rasmussen started a fundamental change in the way Europeans conceived an ideal home. Before the VELUX roof window, nobody really considered an attic or loft as a place one could live! An attic was a 'non-place' used for storage; cold, dark and unattractive. Only children found the attic exciting, with its promise of new discoveries and hidden treasures. As the British musician Edward White remembers from his childhood in the 1920s, *"When I was little, the house had a huge old attic. It was dark and mysterious, and could only be entered through a trap door, with stairs that folded down from the ceiling. Going up stairs that were normally never there, through an almost invisible door in the ceiling, was cool enough by itself; but there were also creepy corners, and cobwebs, and rickety rafters. Who knew what secret treasures might be up there, just waiting to be explored and discovered! They said it was too dirty and dangerous up there, which of course made me want to go even more!"*

To implement such a fundamental change in the concept of suitable living space, VELUX understood at a very early stage the need to communicate with the potential end-users and to explain in detail how they could actually use this forlorn and unattractive space. The brochures exemplified the message in detail with texts and attractive illustrations as in this text from a French brochure from 1959:
"You don't have enough space in your home?
The small family didn't have enough room in the house that once made Mum and Dad so happy when they bought it a dozen years ago. ... It was so tiresome for the father of the family when he came home tired from work in the evening to hear the records being played by the kids. And it was no fun for the mother to see the big boys' toys all over the dining room.

Vous n'avez pas assez de place dans votre maison?

A new generation of parents wanted more space in their homes in order to create children's rooms. Earlier, children were not allotted a room of their own.

A consequence of the new opportunities offered by VELUX was a 'do-it-yourself' boom in the reconstruction of roofs and attics that grew up all over Europe.

So what to do?

Would they have to sell the house? No, they thought about it and found they had room in the attic. All that space where there was nothing but suitcases, skis etc.

In the photographs you can see what the family has done with all this space (and we must point out that it was mother who was most active – she is the one responsible for the well-being of the family and knows how to profit from a little more space)..."

New dreams for new consumers

VELUX understood that the new needs had to be seen from a radically new point of view: from the angle of the 'consumer', not only from the angle of the construction industry. The concept of a 'consumer' was so completely new to Europe that the actual word did not appear in many European languages until very late in the 1950s and the early 1960s. Perhaps one of the reasons for this far-sightedness was that the founder, Mr Villum Kann Rasmussen, was himself the proud father of four children and part of this new generation of parents.

The major target group, the young families, easily identified with the family pattern in the innovative brochures. They certainly aspired to a lifestyle like the one described there, where the father was the breadwinner and the mother the service provider and carer, with the children as the new focus of family life.

But VELUX sold them more than just roof windows. They sold them the potential fulfilment of new, powerful dream images of a different family structure and everyday life. The new dream images focused on space for the children where they could be accepted as equal members of the family, on space for hygiene and wellness, space for the emotions in the relationship of the married couple and for the well-being provided by living in daylight.

Dream images are the images people have in their minds about how life should be when it is really good. Images of what it means to be a good parent, to be a good partner in a relationship, what it is like to be young, what a good workplace is and what a good future should be. Dream images are not reality. They are ideal images that we use as guidelines every time we make a choice.

The content of these dream images changed even though the words remained the same: 'a good home', 'a good relationship' suddenly meant something different. At certain times, the con-

18

The new 'baby boom' after the Second World War
became a focus for the new generation of parents.
The amount of toys in these children's rooms from
the 1950s may seem limited to a contemporary
generation, but at the time it was an exorbitant
dream attained by few.

From the early years, VELUX understood the new
dreams of family life. Here, one of the first examples
in advertising of a father enjoying spending time
with his children – 40 years ahead of time in its
thinking!

tent seemed to change drastically and very quickly. One of these drastic changes in the content of dream images of what a good life should be like took place in the 1950s.

The democratic VELUX concept

From the first appearance on the market of VELUX windows, information leaflets targeted both the construction industry and the new 'consumers'. The product range and pricing were open and clear to all the interested parties, something unheard of before in the business. The first 'democratic' window concept had been born.

In focusing primarily on the customer's needs and dreams, not just on the product, the company was a good forty years ahead of its time in its forward-looking thinking and its understanding of the market. The new consumers definitely liked the new democratic concept of the roof windows and the independence and empowerment it gave them ('empowerment' was another word that had to wait many years before appearing in the European languages).

New concepts of the home

So many new children's rooms were constructed in family homes that a whole new generation of Europeans grew up with a different view of attic space and living in daylight. To them, a home without roof windows and daylight was almost unthinkable. Much later examples of the consequences of this change in the perception of the home can be seen in the following chapters of this book. VELUX really did change the European way of living.

Bathroom dreams

Europeans benefited from the explosive economic growth of the 1960s as industrialisation really took off. Large groups joined the wealthier middle class. Much of their economic surplus was invested in better, larger homes. The first priority was space for new children's rooms. But second on the list of priorities was a new bathroom. Attitudes to hygiene were changing towards a greater concern for personal cleanliness, and even fifty years ago this was very different from our concepts of acceptable hygiene today.

Back then, in the 1960s, the daily personal hygiene routine usually consisted of washing your face and hands with a cloth

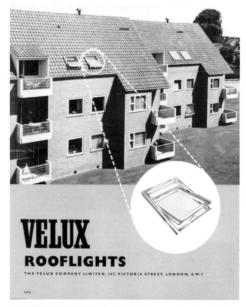

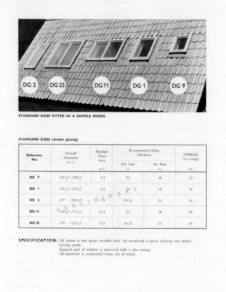

The very first brochures from VELUX also made the price list available to the end-user, the 'consumer'.

The dream images of a relationship between husband and wife changed drastically from 1959 to 1999, from service to emotions. And so did the VELUX communication to customers.

and water in the morning, perhaps brushing your teeth, combing your hair and, for the men, shaving. Soap was a luxury. Most people did all this at the kitchen sink. Bathing or showering was something you did once a week at most, involving loud protests from the children; and since half of all homes in many countries had no separate bathroom, you often had to bathe at the public baths. Hair was rarely washed, since hairdressers and barbers advised that it was bad to do it too often: every three or four weeks was the norm. The prevailing concept of the limited need for personal hygiene is evident from the minute toilets/bathrooms built in the many flats constructed in the new housing blocks for families with children. They usually consisted of two rooms, a narrow kitchen and a toilet with no bathtub or shower stall, but with a washbasin with a showerhead attached.

When VELUX showed their new bathroom dreams in their brochures, they fed straight into a new and growing need: the luxury of personal hygiene, even the possibility of a bath becoming a daily event!

This dream vision bathroom was a hitherto unattainable luxury for many Europeans in 1954.

Family life: you, me and us
Visions of the function of family life changed drastically between the 1950s and the 1990s: from being a practical solution to everyday life, it became a predominantly emotional contract. In 1950 a woman needed a financial provider and a man needed a practical service helper. Parenting was generally the woman's job. Love in a relationship was nice, but not absolutely necessary – practical aspects counted for more.

The fundamental dream images of relationships, of gender roles, of parenthood, changed drastically and had huge consequences. Women entered the labour market in large numbers. And then their daughters and granddaughters became better and better educated, so that by the beginning of the new millennium, young women were in the majority in higher education in all European countries. And from the beginning of the new millennium, young men redefined masculinity drastically. The new fathers saw themselves as more masculine in their proud fatherhood than earlier generations of men, who had left the child-caring responsibilities to their wives.

This fundamental shift in the content of dream images has not led to the demise of family life. On the contrary, family life has

Young women's dream images changed drastically in the 1970s, and VELUX expressed this change in its advertising. (1976)

A masculine home in 1978 had dark, classical English country-house style, but daylight dreams sneaked in.

Customers of today want much more daylight in their homes than earlier generations.

never been more important. But the dream images of the new generations of families are about emotional values, not practical solutions. You choose your partner for love, not because you need a cook or a provider. Children have become symbols of family happiness and are increasingly the centre of attention.

Married couples used to call each other 'Mum' or 'Dad', but this is unthinkable for the new generations. Now they are individuals in their own right. Great mums and dads, yes, but to their children. For each other, they expect to be lovers.

These changed roles in family life can be seen in the growing need for married couples to create 'spaces of their own' away from their children. And this has meant a new search for space in the home, often resulting in the use of an attic space for great bedrooms and bathrooms, and the installation of many roof windows – since they also dream of living in more and more daylight. In this book, we show many examples of this new focus.

Living in daylight – more and more daylight!

Right from the beginning, Mr Villum Kann Rasmussen understood the importance of daylight in the home. But it would be decades before consumers really shared his views. To most people, a roof window was a way of solving the practical problem of creating more space. Over time the customers' perceptions changed; and as a consequence, roof windows are now primarily seen as ways of creating daylight-filled rooms, and secondly of solving practical problems.

Changing
the home

Changing the home

The first generation of Europeans to change their homes by installing a single VELUX window in new children's rooms in the attic started a fundamental change in the concept of what a home should look like. As their children grew up, these new generations wanted more daylight in their homes, much more daylight. And even though fewer and fewer children were being born to families all over Europe, they wanted bigger children's rooms, more and bigger bathrooms, new home workplaces and integrated kitchens and living rooms. And as the baby boomers became parents themselves, they too wanted more space and more daylight and once again wanted to change their old homes.

For all these generations, it was a matter of course that they could decide and choose according to their own visions. This chapter visits people all over Europe who have chosen to change their homes to live better in daylight. They live in very different houses, built in different styles in different periods. But despite the apparent differences, they all have one thing in common: their wish to change an old house into a contemporary, light-filled framework for their daily life. They have realised their dreams of more space and more daylight, of higher ceilings, of bigger kitchen/living rooms, of larger children's rooms, and of inside/outside rooms opening up to beautiful natural surroundings or gardens.

People across Europe have opened their doors to give us a glimpse of how they have changed their homes, letting in more daylight. They live in the cities of Amsterdam, Aarhus and Tallin, in suburbs of Paris and Copenhagen, in small towns in Brittany and England and in villages in Switzerland, Portugal and Germany.

They all have their own stories of the process of change, and they have all been asked the same two questions: where is their favourite place in the home, and what do they particularly like doing at weekends. Their answers offer amazing insights into the similarities and varieties of European living in daylight.

"My favourite place at home is in the light-filled family room in the attic. I meditate there every morning; it just gives me so much energy - especially during the winter months when it's really grey here in The Netherlands. When it's raining, I sometimes just lounge in the comfortable chairs with a good book. Actually, the whole family loves it up here. We're practically never in the big living room downstairs on the first floor any more."

An illuminated darkroom: Jordaan, Amsterdam, Netherlands

The old darkroom in the attic before the change.

"At first, when we bought this old town house with four floors, we just didn't consider using the attic space. We fell in love with the incredible light in all the well-proportioned rooms of the house. Here in old Amsterdam, the town houses have very tall windows. And our house has windows on three sides," says Elisabeth Merle Petersen, who lives with her husband Kees and the children Julius and Lideweg in one of the oldest parts of Amsterdam, the Jordaan. Originally from Denmark, Elisabeth has enjoyed living in The Netherlands since she met Kees.

The house is an old coach house dating back to the 1600s, when it was used for parking the coaches and horses of the rich merchant family living in a huge mansion on the other side of the courtyard with an imposing façade out to the canal-street behind. The old coach-and-horse stable at street level is the entrance for the Merle Petersen family; it has huge doors opening to the street and a height of five metres to the ceiling. The family's bicycles are parked in the entrance, and Elisabeth has created an inspiring office space there for her business as a trend-spotter and interior decorator. Kees owns a company that produces sounds for commercials and films. "He has a great job," Elisabeth

"At weekends, weather permitting, I love being in our tiny garden and second house in one of the parks in the centre of Amsterdam. I've changed it from dilapidated to really romantic: lots of roses and even an outdoor bath. Kees bought it for me when he asked me to marry him. We go there by bicycle, and the kids enjoy it too."

The kitchen on the second floor is a huge, pleasant, light-filled room with plenty of space for lounging in the corner sofas, and seats at least twelve guests around the big table.

smiles. "We're always scouting for new voice talents, so we go out a lot to theatres, restaurants and bars. Amsterdam is a very lively city with lots of culture."

Originally the upstairs floors were used as the kitchen for the merchant house and as accommodation for all the servants. Today the kitchen is a huge, pleasant, light-filled room with ample space for lounging in the corner sofas and seats at least twelve guests around the big table.

"At first we lived in a small house not far from here – it was only 80 m² – which we restored completely ourselves: bathroom, kitchen, everything. When our children arrived, the space felt too limited and we were lucky to be able to buy this town house of 360 m² from an old photographer. Throughout the long history of the house, many artists lived here – you can feel the house has a creative atmosphere," Elisabeth says. "You have to listen to the rooms when you want to change them. What do they require from us to be welcoming? I believe if we take good care of the house, the house will take good care of us!"

Elisabeth and Kees designed all the changes, but this time they had builders helping with the work. After restoring and changing the interior of the house over two years, the Merle Petersens found that the house also needed a new roof.

"That was when we discovered the possibilities of the old photographer's darkroom, the attic," Elisabeth smiles. "We installed ten great roof windows, opening up the attic on both sides. Now we have a light-filled family room with a view all around over the roofs, terraces and courtyards of old Amsterdam. We can even see the green copper dome of the Lutheran Church.

The Merle Petersen home in old Amsterdam is in a narrow, cobbled street, but is open on three sides to the large yard at the back. The many roof windows in the new roof let in fabulous daylight and give the family views of the green dome of the Lutheran Church.

Today the old coach-and-horse stable at street level is the entrance for the Merle Petersen family. It has tall doors opening to the street and a height of five metres to the ceiling. The family bicycles are parked there.

Countryside views: Barnfields, Staffordshire Moorlands, England

The architect Adam Wardle inherited an old sandstone cottage in Staffordshire, and he was very pleased with the cosy traditional home with small rooms and windows and a dark attic. But he imagined that some day the plain sandstone cottage could perhaps be transformed into a stunning new home with a spectacular view of the surrounding countryside.

After ten years of living in the cottage, the family wanted to realise its potential for a different way of living, with much more space, daylight and openness. As in many other countries in Europe, the local authorities required any building work to be in harmony with neighbouring properties, so all the changes were planned in close collaboration with the Staffordshire Moorlands District Council. Planners were generally supportive of the project, although they asked for the changes to the original façade to be subtle and to complement the neighbouring cottages.

Adam and his wife Julia began the renovation project by demolishing the whole building, apart from one wall, and then added more space in an innovative way. "My wife Julia and I realised that, with an extension and a mezzanine floor, we could

With a combination of roof windows and large glazed doors, the whole south-facing rear of the house, including the living room and conservatory, offers stunning views over the fields and hills of Staffordshire while letting in abundant daylight.

"My favourite place at home is immediately inside the front door because as soon as I enter, the light, the views and the sense of space creates calm and restores the soul."

"On sunny Sundays we like to open all the doors at the rear of the house and let the house be one with the garden."

The Staffordshire Moorlands when the heather is in bloom – a spectacular experience in purple which Adam and Julia enjoy from their living room.

double the size of our home. And by placing twelve roof windows above the extension and the mezzanine, we brought the outside indoors – and the feeling of being bathed in natural light works wonders for the mood of the place."

The interior of the cottage is essentially open-plan. But the design ensures that it does not feel like one large open space. "I wanted the house to be a flexible collection of spaces that could be opened or closed depending on the season or what we are using it for. I also wanted to make the most of the natural daylight. With a combination of roof windows and large glazed doors, the whole south-facing rear of the house, including the living room and conservatory, offers stunning views over the fields and hills of Staffordshire. When coming through the front door, the first thing you see is a view straight out on to the landscape. The entire rear of the house can also be opened up to the countryside," says Adam.

A large insulated wooden door has also been incorporated into the design. On winter nights this can easily slide shut to close off the conservatory, making the kitchen and dining area more intimate. "The door is intended to replicate an original barn door," says Julia – acknowledging the rich history of the cottage, which was originally an 18th-century hay barn. A similar hint of the past is noticeable on the exterior, which uses reclaimed stone and tiles from the original cottage.

A stunning feature is the reinforced glass bridge that links the upstairs landing with the master bedroom. This gives you a view of the sky from the floor below. As Adam puts it, "the glass bridge acts as a sort of drawbridge to the private quarters." Across the glass bridge on the mezzanine level is the master bedroom itself. This is light and airy, with roof windows offering fantastic views of the sprawling countryside.

42

Living in a cowhouse: Bauernhof Adler, Erftstadt, Rhein-Erftkreis, Germany

"Why not move into the countryside?" Martina Gladbach and Herbert Adler thought when their old house in an attractive part of the city of Cologne seemed to have turned into an obstacle course after the arrival of two small sons: up the stairs, down the stairs with the babies' pushchairs, shopping bags and heavy water bottles. So they went looking for a house in the countryside that could be converted into an optimal family home with lots of large, light-filled rooms – and not too many stairs!

They decided on a 100-year-old former cowhouse and hayloft in the village of Erfstadt and undertook the enormous task of changing it into their ideal of a home.

Today, a wealth of windows let in abundant daylight and offer views of the surrounding countryside. Downstairs is an open kitchen/living space where the family enjoys entertaining guests. They also have a guest room there so visitors do not have to drive back to the city after a good dinner.

On the upstairs floor, each of the two small boys has his own room with a view of the countryside; and Martina and Herbert have created a large 'well-being and wellness zone' all for them-

Martina and Herbert retained the old structures of the cowhouse with uncovered, rough brick walls and timber frames as decorative elements complementing the modern furniture and simple style.

The open kitchen/living room downstairs in the renovated, old cowhouse caters for plenty of room to play in for the two small, active boys.

selves: a spacious bedroom with an en suite closet and luxurious bathroom area. They enjoy this as much as the French family in Brittany visited later in this chapter.

The whole attic area is airy and filled with daylight from fourteen roof windows. Electrical operation of windows and sunscreens makes regulation of the indoor climate an easy task.

Martina and Herbert both work in Cologne, 25 km away. They enjoy the quiet, idyllic life of the countryside with their sons as a contrast to the hustle and bustle of the city.

When the reconstruction of the old cowhouse was being done, their neighbours certainly wondered what was happening when they saw the young couple had decided to leave the rough bricks of the walls untreated, since they liked the contrast with the open architecture and the hypermodern design. Martina and Herbert still remember fondly when the village was invited to see their house on the inside for the first time, and a neighbour asked in surprise, "Is that what they call gastronomy now?" on seeing the former cowhouse changed into the huge, open living room/kitchen.

A neighbour asked in surprise, "Is that what they call gastronomy now?" on seeing the rough brick walls and the hypermodern design kitchen.

"We already have two favourite places in our house: one for summer and a very cosy one for winter when it is so unpleasantly cold, wet and windy outside. In the summertime, we often spend the whole day on the terrace by the pool. In winter, we light the big fire in the middle of our large living room."

"Both places have lots of space to play in for the children and for reading and relaxing for us. Both offer unimpeded views of the beautiful landscapes of the countryside where we live. And the large French windows in the living room also let in daylight and air when we want it."

The new extension to the house has been incorporated in the natural forest of fir trees. The colourful wooden façade was Tiina Paet's idea.

The capital of Estonia, Tallin, is a picturesque city with a medieval centre.

A minister at home: Tallin, Nomme, Estonia

Right in the centre of the romantic, historic capital of Estonia, Tallin, you find the green district of Nomme. Roads are small, trees and gardens allow for lively bird life, and a strangely silent and undisturbed atmosphere gives you the illusion of being in the countryside.

Here a young family, the Paets, has just completed the extension of their house. Before this they lived in an apartment, but they dreamed of having their own house – "to be by ourselves" – because living so close to the neighbours sometimes seemed just too much. They enjoy the neighbourhood of Nomme: "The kids like it here, they can be outside and there are lots of other kids in the neighbourhood," Tiina Paet says.

Having found the beautiful plot, they built their first house with an area of 80 m² nine years ago, but when their two daughters, Sylvia and Olivia, arrived, the house just became too small. So they set out to extend it to twice the size, 160 m².

This story might seem similar to that of many other young families all over Europe, but in one respect this family is rather unusual: the father of the two young girls, Urmas Paet, is the Minister of Foreign Affairs in Estonia. Few ministers of foreign

affairs have small children, but another unusual aspect is that Paet is a very young man, born in 1974. The job rarely leaves him much time at home, but whenever he is there, this is the place where he relaxes and enjoys family life. "Sometimes I regret having a job like this. But it's not forever," the young minister says.

One of the reasons why the Paets chose to live in Nomme was the environment, with bird song and country air. So when they started to build the house, they tried to spare as many trees as possible. Some pines are even integrated into the terrace. Furnishing and designing the house was enjoyable: the colourful part of the house was designed by Tiina. The colourful stripes of the wooden façade were mixed and matched with the landscape and surroundings and this is a detail Urmas Paet particularly likes. Another favourite is the hallway with lots of daylight and a glass door with a big house number.

The only room that rather surprised Urmas Paet was the brown, white and orange bathroom chosen by his wife. "It was very strange at first. But I'm getting used to it."

The minister walks out on the morning terrace and takes a look at the still unfinished garden. "There is peace and quiet here. Yes, I can say this is a perfect home!"

"My favourite place at home is the light-filled entrance. The windows let the daylight into our house and it feels as if the trees outside are inside our house too."

"At weekends, when I'm at home – which is far too rarely - I just enjoy very much being together with my wife, relaxing and playing with our daughters."

Building blocks of light and shade: Hørsholm, Denmark

"It's incredible what daylight can do to a basically mundane house," says Thomas Kent Larsen, who recently completed a thorough renovation of the family's 1960s house. He had inherited the 136 m² tract house, and at first he and his wife Camilla just painted most of the interior white, but did not really change anything. Like most tract houses built in Denmark during the building boom of the 1960s, it consisted of a large living room, a narrow, windowless corridor with doors opening to tiny children's rooms, a bedroom and a bathroom.

After living in the house for ten years, they felt the need for a change, like the English Wardle family and the French Orpwood family also mentioned in this chapter. With the arrival of their two children, Sophia and Mads Peter, the house felt increasingly cramped. The children's rooms were too small and the kitchen made it impossible to have meals together. The Larsens first thought of adding two new children's rooms, but they could not imagine what to do with the kitchen/living room. Then, at a dinner with friends, they got an eye-opener when they talked to an architect who sketched out completely new possibilities on the table napkin!

"In a big renovation process like ours, it isn't the area in square metres or where you put the flatscreen TV that makes the house exciting. In our house, light and shade are the building blocks."

After a long and hard process of converting the dark family home into a light-filled, open space, Thomas Kent Larsen enjoys the well planned interplay of daylight throughout the house. He documented the renovation process on his webpage in order for others to profit from his experience.

"Lying in the tub in the evening gazing up at the stars in the night sky gives you a splendid feeling of relaxation and well-being," says Camilla Larsen.

After the extension to the house and the new roof structure, the kitchen area is a lovely, bright, open room. To determine the best position of the roof windows, the architect used a daylight laboratory.

The architect continued working with the family. At first he asked them to make a plan for each room in the house: to write down which functions in the house they would give the highest priority and how large they thought the rooms ought to be. Then a very different solution was decided: a kitchen/living room of 42 m^2 with a new ceiling opening up all the way to the ridge beams, bigger children's rooms and a new large window in the end-façade to give the dark corridor light.

One of the points the Larsens wanted changed was the rather dark interior of the house. They wanted much more daylight. So the architect tested a model of the house in the daylight laboratory of the School of Architecture at the Royal Academy in Copenhagen. This resulted in the strategic placing of roof windows to bring light to the darker areas of the house.

Before starting the actual building process, Thomas Kent Larsen decided to share what he had learned with others, creating an internet site where other homeowners could follow the whole design process with a webcam, articles and links. "I wanted to show others how to exploit the potential of tract houses from the 1960s and 1970s by giving them access to useful advice on how to get through the whole renovation process," says Thomas Kent Larsen, who had himself felt a great lack of this kind of inspiration.

"In a big renovation process like ours, it isn't the area in square metres or where you put the flatscreen TV that makes the house exciting. In our house, light and shade are the building blocks," says Thomas Kent Larsen.

"Our favourite place is our open kitchen/living room. It's a daylight-suffused, splendid, tall room, which is the central spot in the house."

"At weekends, we like to take small trips. However, since our baby arrived recently, our weekend trips are rather short and mainly to the beautiful surroundings of Buchs."

The barn for three generations: Buchs, Zürich, Switzerland

Like many other Europeans, a young Swiss couple, Christian and Nicole Bühler, both working in downtown Zürich, wanted to live in the countryside after their son Mael was born. The Bühlers found a solution to their dream in a farmhouse belonging to Nicole's grandfather, Gottfried Meier, just outside the village of Buchs in the wine district of Zürich. Far enough out to be real countryside, yet close enough to commute to Zürich without too much hassle.

Nicole's grandfather still lives in his old farmhouse. He used to be a farmer like his own father before him, who originally built the farmhouse more than a hundred years ago. Gottfried Meier gave the house to his grandchild, wanting to continue living in the house for the rest of his life.

Before the three generations – grandfather, granddaughter with her husband and a great-grandson – could move into the house and live together, they had to find out if it was at all possible to rebuild the old house to create more living space inside the old walls. This led to many discussions with the local authority about the strict building restrictions that were meant to preserve the village appearance of Buchs. Like the families in

The Swiss family enjoys the way roof windows placed one on top of the other in the stairwells bring daylight to the whole house.

Nicole's grandfather still lives in his old farmhouse. It's good for Mael to have Granddad living so close, especially now when a little sister has arrived.

Nicole and Christian Bühler had a baby daughter, Alene, after moving to Buchs, where they share the house of her grandfather, the farmer Gottfried Meier.

The Bühlers found a solution to their dream in the farmhouse belonging to Nicole's grandfather just outside the village of Buchs in the wine district of Zürich. Far enough out to be real countryside, yet close enough to commute to Zürich without too much hassle.

Croatia and England visited in this chapter, the Bühlers worked in close cooperation with the council. They found a solution that convinced the local authority of the best way of keeping the old building alive.

Together with an architect, they developed a concept that opened up the inside of the house by using roof windows. The former living section of the house was to keep its structure, while the old two-storey stable would become a huge living room – the new family focus for the three generations!

> "My favourite place at home is the garden, that's why I wanted to see it from the windows of the new upper floor."

Parents' delight: Paris, France

When Pascal Corticchiato and his wife Christine chose to buy this house in 1998, the main reasons were its closeness to Paris in an area they liked, and the three spacious upstairs bedrooms. With two small daughters, it was just perfect. But soon they had three daughters who were not so small any more, and the house felt cramped.

Moving to a new house did not seem an attractive option – because Pascal's parents and Christine's work were nearby, because of the girls' schools and because of the garden that Pascal had come to love so much. The solution of using the attic for children's rooms was not really feasible because of the W-truss of the roof construction. So they made a radical decision: to raise the roof and create a whole new floor – a floor strictly for their own use, leaving the three bedrooms and the bathroom on the second floor for the three daughters, Mélodie, Clémentine and Valentine.

Pascal envisaged being able to see his favourite place, the beautiful garden, from his bed; so he planned for façade windows in the dwarf wall in combination with lots of roof windows in the ceiling. "I had a hard time convincing the builders to cut the

The terraced house in a Parisian suburb had a whole new attic floor added.

"My favourite place at home is the garden, that's why I wanted to see it from the windows of the new upper floor," Pascal says.

The view of Pascal's beloved garden is just as he imagined it.

Youngest daughter, Valentine, enjoys that the 'parents only' rule for the new top floor is not strictly applied.

insulation material and to place the many windows that way, but when they saw the result, they agreed the idea was brilliant and now they recommend a similar solution to other people rebuilding their houses," Pascal says.

The result of the long, hard building process is an upper floor with a large, bright bedroom filled with the ever-changing daylight, even on the many grey days so prevalent in Paris during the winter. The view of Pascal's beloved garden is just as he imagined it.

A bathroom with a bubbly spa bathtub was built too – but not used as often as they thought they would – as well as a guest room and a small home office for Christine to work on her computer. But now that it is there, she mainly uses it to check the weather forecast and so it is usually occupied by the girls – the 'parents only' rule is not that strictly applied.

"This floor is the same size as our very first apartment in Paris," Pascal says. "We really enjoy the feeling of having a place of our own!"

The garden is a small green oasis of 300 m². Surrounded by bamboo and trees, it is a completely secluded, private place despite the closeness to the neighbours. Pascal has built a small goldfish pond and a bird bath. He has a dream of enlarging the garden, perhaps buying a piece of the neighbour's garden and then creating an outdoor kitchen.

"At weekends, I love staying at home in my garden. The car is not touched from Friday to Monday. Home is like being in the countryside - nice, relaxing! The sound of frogs from the pond, the dragonflies hovering in the air and the neighbour's cat trying to catch the goldfish. And at weekends we really like taking a siesta in the new bedroom that we have all to ourselves!"

"After having moved into our new house, we changed our lifestyle. We like the evenings very much: when the kids go to their rooms, we go upstairs into our living room and talk. Now we know how much influence a house and its architecture have on family life."

Teenagers in the house: Lake Bled, Slovenia

Near the Slovenian capital of Ljubljana, a young family with two kids lived in an apartment of 80 m². The place worked fine for several years, until their daughter started going to school, when she definitely no longer wanted to share a room with her elder brother!

So, like many other young Europeans, the family started to look for solutions. At first they considered building a completely new house, but the time and expense involved were not attractive prospects. Both were busy with their careers and could not take the time off to go through a lengthy building process. Instead, they decided to buy an old house and then renovate it.

After house-hunting for a long time and considering several options, they decided on a house near the beautiful Lake Bled. It had the advantage of being big enough to divide into separate sections for the kids and for the parents. For inspiration on how to change the house, the family visited a building fair in Ljubljana where they saw photos of different possibilities at the VELUX stand which they really liked. So the family started discussing their wishes and needs with an architect.

Their former flat was a very traditional one with average-size

Near the spectacular Lake Bled in Slovenia, an old house was changed to meet new needs.

66

To let in maximum daylight, the family installed 23 roof windows in the reconstruction of the attic floor, even on the outside where two windows were installed in the roof over the balcony, since the projecting roof is very wide and does not let in enough daylight.

The whole upper floor of the house is the parents' zone.

windows, small pokey rooms and many doors. In the new house the family wanted a contemporary concept with open spaces and a lot of daylight on the ground floor as well as in the attic.

To manage the whole reconstruction process, the family hired an architect, and together with him they drew up a plan they really liked. The basic concept of the house was that the ground floor would be designed as an open space containing the kitchen as well as dining and living room areas. Another part of the ground floor was to house two large children's rooms and a bathroom.

To let in maximum light, the family installed 23 roof windows in the reconstruction of the attic floor – even on the outside, where two windows are installed in the roof of the covered balcony, since it does not let enough daylight in to the balcony.

Realising it would not be many years before the children reached their teens, they also catered for the needs of the future: the whole attic was to be reserved for the parents – their bedroom, their bathroom and an open living room. Like the Corticchiato family in Paris, they now very much enjoy having a space of their own – and so do the teenagers!

"Our weekends are also quite different from when we lived in a small flat; in the summer, we are all around the house and in winter we spend a lot of time on the attic floor as we have a beautiful view of the mountains from there."

"My favourite place at home is the kitchen, because of its lovely daylight and high ceiling, and because it provides a lot of workspace – every aspect a constant source of nourishment for family life and crea- tivity."

Kitchen garage: Birkerød, Denmark

When the Hoff family decided to change their old house from the 1950s, what they wanted most of all was a new kitchen. Their old kitchen felt closed-in like a cigar box, because the walls and the very low ceiling were covered in old, darkened wooden pan- elling. Lena and Michael Hoff live with their two boys, Mathias and Lucas, in Birkerød, 20 km outside the city of Copenhagen. Most people living in Birkerød commute to Copenhagen like Lena and Michael. Birkerød is more or less a suburb of the city, with the advantage of lovely lakes and woods nearby. It is a safe, green place for their children to live.

The task of changing the basically sound but old-fashioned house into the family's dream vision of space and light was defi- nitely not an easy one. A solution was found by completely in- corporating a garage/workshop, originally added to the house in the 1970s.

To their great surprise they found a structure of beautiful and unusual roof rafters when they opened up the low ceiling. The ceiling was completely removed and a new one constructed right up to the centre beam, giving the new kitchen a height of al- most four metres at the tallest point. To let in daylight, four new

The ceiling of the former garage was completely removed and a new one constructed right up to the centre beam, giving the new kitchen a height of almost four metres at the tallest point. To let in daylight, four new roof windows were installed.

roof windows were installed. The floor was completely dug up to make room for new water and electricity pipes.

"Our new kitchen is suffused with light and air from morning to night," Lena Hoff says. "Now we're always in the kitchen. It has become our Command Centre. Every morning we coordinate the tasks of the day there, and we always end up there in the evenings. This is where our kids, two and four years old, play games; it's the place for having dinner with friends, and it's here we have our heart-to-heart talks."

"At weekends, I like opening the doors to the garden, enjoying the smell of the grass and the flowers right in the kitchen, listening to the birds and letting in the sunlight."

Siamese twins: Zagreb, Šestine, Croatia

A close neighbour to the Croatian capital of Zagreb, the protected nature park Medvednica is covered in beautiful natural forests. It is a favourite recreational area for the citizens of Zagreb, offering numerous hiking trails and accommodation for climbers, several historic sites, interesting caves, an old mine and other attractions.

So it is no wonder that a Croatian family with a grown-up daughter immediately took up the challenge when they had the unique opportunity to reconstruct two small, old houses on the outskirts of Zagreb in Šestine, right on the edge of a hill with a sweeping panoramic view overlooking the Medvednica park and Zagreb.

It was not an easy challenge, since Šestine is an old, protected village with its own architecture and style. Creative vision was needed to create a solution for comfortable contemporary living with a maximum of free views of the surrounding landscape and the charmingly placed houses on the hills.

The shape of the new house follows the shape of the previous buildings. Where the twin houses were, a complex of houses is now placed like Siamese twins: separate but connected. The lower part is the home of the parents and the upper, separate apartment is for their daughter.

The lower part of the house is laid out as a completely open space containing the kitchen and the dining room. Stairs lead down to the living room with spectacular panoramic views of the surrounding area.

The large, new kitchen extends into the living room downstairs. This lower part of the twin houses is the home for the elder generation while the younger generation lives in the upper house.

74

Two small, old houses on a sloping ground were joined to create homes for two generations. Each house has its own facilities while catering for family life together when desired.

"My favourite place in our home is the living room. As we have a young orchard next to our house, the roof windows make it possible for us to enjoy the leaves budding and the wonderful blossoming in spring."

"On Sundays we like to spend time with our 8-month-old granddaughter. She really enjoys playing on her bedding on the floor and looking through the roof windows at floating clouds and changes between sun and rain. Looking at her while she is learning about the world around her is a real pleasure."

A bathroom with a view: Le Conquet, Brittany, France

An all-round view of the sea from a bathroom window is a scenery many people dream of, but few ever get the chance to have: the port of le Conquet, with its sailing and fishing boats, piers, tidal estuary, dunes, rocks and cliffs and the Atlantic Ocean stretching into the distance, is a unique location. Even on a grey day in Brittany, the light is dazzling and the view stunning. Le Conquet is a picture-postcard fishing village on the westernmost tip of France in the county of Finistère, which literally means 'the end of the world'. Nestled in a north-facing harbour, it still hosts an active fleet of fishing boats. Far from the noise and bustle of Paris (more than 600 km), this is the haven where the French/English family, the Orpwoods, have chosen to live. By restoring an imposing stone house, they have made their dream of owning an elegant, stylish family home come true.

When the Orpwoods bought the 100-year-old house back in 1985, its classic features – high ceilings with stucco, panelled walls, large arched windows, cosy fireplaces and a sculptured staircase – were not much in demand. But they knew this was just what they had always wanted: a house with a genuine soul and lots of space.

First they restored the two main floors of the house to their

The new attic floor has a bedroom, bathroom, shower stall and dressing room in one open plan. Roof windows on both sides of the sloping roof allow daylight to penetrate from all angles. And just like other couples in this chapter, Rolande and Glynn Orpwood enjoy their private wellness space.

An all-round view of the sea is a scenery many people dream of, but few ever get the chance to have. The Orpwoods have a fabulous view from their new terrace created by the roof windows: the port of le Conquet, with its sailing and fishing boats, piers, tidal estuary, dunes, rocks and cliffs, and stretching into the distance, the Atlantic Ocean.

81

The old Breton captain's mansion has been lovingly restored into a contemporary home. A long row of Cabrio roof windows creates a spacious balcony allowing the family to enjoy the spectacular Breton sea views.

original beauty while updating the practical, convenience aspects. Fifteen years and a son later, they started thinking about how to make the most of the top floor. The house had plenty of rooms, certainly enough for a small family, but because of the unique view of the estuary they loved so much, they needed to find a solution that would make the most of the view without destroying the classic lines of the house.

Changing the loft from a storeroom into a combined bedroom/bathroom took a lot of planning. They wanted every detail to be of the highest standard, and even though professional builders did the actual work, they were intensely involved in the design. The bathroom is made from warm Doussie hardwood with an eye for even the smallest detail. In the shower, for example, there is a ship's porthole window offering a delightful view of the ever-changing tidal estuary, even while you are taking a shower! A state-of-the-art music system is installed too. Their almost grown-up son enjoys this, as he plays in a band and is passionate about music.

Since the main aim of this transformation was to open the space up to as much of the fantastic sea view as possible, a solution had to be found. However, building a roof terrace would have spoilt the classic design of the old house. So they chose to install four VELUX Cabrio windows side by side, which all open up to create a small terrace when deployed, but which still look like roof windows from the outside when closed.

The transformation was just stunning. A north/west-oriented room completely saturated with warm daylight and the enchanting view of the sea as the backdrop. "Our living room faces north, so even if it's very bright because of the big windows, it can be rather cold downstairs. So I often go up here to read," Rolande Orpwood says.

"My favourite place at home is the attic floor because I love the sea views and it's always so bright and warm up here. At weekends we enjoy the beautiful surroundings, kayaking, sailing or going for a stroll. Glyn goes jogging along the coast and I cycle or we both just lounge about at home."

"We are very interested in French cuisine and of course French wines. Glyn is a member of a wine club that organises wine tastings once a month and an annual visit to the vineyards for several days. On Sundays we enjoy a really lovely meal and choosing the wines to go with it – it's such a great pleasure."

Back to the future: Aarhus, Denmark

Many a middle-aged man takes it as a fact of life that interior decorating is really his wife's concern and responsibility, not his. But what happens if he gets divorced? After a divorce, where will he live? What is his home going to look like? Does he really want to take memorabilia with him from a part of his life that is now over?

Moving from a huge house filled with antiques, feminine silverware and decorative items in an upmarket neighbourhood close to the capital, John Andersen found a solution after his divorce, and bought his mother's former house in Aarhus, the second-largest city in Denmark.

He set out reconstructing the interior in an inventive style with open spaces. The rather small, unprepossessing house from the 1940s with a total of 100 m² on four floors is now an elegant, very masculine-style home with absolutely no knick-knacks, frills, candles or flowery wraps. Instead there are just a few distinctive pieces by classical furniture designers like Eames, Kjærholm and Wegner.

"All I have to consider now is myself and my needs, so I can do exactly as I want," John Andersen says. He was born and grew up

The redbrick house is an architectural oyster: from the outside shell you cannot see the pearl behind the façade.

84

John Andersen's favourite place in the house is his study in the attic. He is an architectural designer and his worktable is right under the roof windows, allowing him to work with his designs in daylight.

"My favourite place at home is relaxing in the Sting Ray chair in the small mezzanine; from there I have a beautiful view of Aarhus – and of my desk – through the roof windows."

in the house, but has lived elsewhere all of his adult life. However, the freedom to decide everything initially left him rather clueless about the solutions he wanted, so he contacted an architect.

"Many of his suggestions I would never even have imagined even in my wildest dreams," John Andersen says. "For example, I hadn't imagined at all that the attic floor could be used for anything sensible, as it was small, dark and pokey." Walls were taken down, a small mezzanine was created and a number of new windows were installed in the roof.

"The attic is where I spend most time in the house now," says John Andersen. Renovating and reconstructing the house really has been a huge task, because literally everything had to be renewed: floors, doors and windows, the kitchen and the bathroom.

"It's really been worthwhile reconstructing the house, because every day I enjoy my minimalist home. I can't think of anything I would have done in a different way."

"I don't have a favourite place in the house yet. In the evening, I particularly enjoy sitting by the pool listening to the vast silence here."

Back to the village in luxury: Quinta de Aldeia, Avanca, Portugal

Manuel Vaz da Silva does a lot of travelling in his job as a civil engineer. Based in Lisbon, the capital of Portugal, his job frequently takes him to South America, Angola and northern Europe. But his heart is in the small village of Avanca 60 km south of Oporto; not because of any distinctive beauty there, since the surrounding area is flat agricultural land quite far from the Atlantic Ocean; but because he was born there. He left at the early age of ten to get a better education than the four years of schooling that were offered to children at the time in villages like Avanca. For all of his adult life he has been based in Lisbon, but now he spends as much time as possible in his country house, the 'Quinta de Aldeia', which he has had lovingly and extensively restored. When it came up for sale, he had fierce competition from the local priest, but he won – perhaps because of the tenacity acquired in his youth as president of Benfica, the famous football club.

Manuel Vaz da Silva has every intention of moving to Avanca some day. "Not now, I'm far too busy in my business, but later I'll definitely move!" Instead, he comes to the Quinta on most weekends.

The country house is a large complex and its everyday running

The old manorhouse has had a large, new guests' wing added with facilities for banquets. Also, completely new horse stables were added as horses are Manuel da Silva's passion. The rare white lippizaner is his favourite.

90

When Manuel da Silva bought the old Portuguese manorhouse, he found it almost too huge and as he only used a minute part for himself, he thought, why not change it into a guest house? The main house has six guest suites under the roof, several more on the grounds, and offers a range of leisure activities like horse back riding and horsecart driving.

is entrusted to Erol, without whom the enormous process of re-building and restructuring would never have succeeded. He was the man who oversaw the project of changing the old Quinta into a luxurious country guest house, a process that took more than a year.

"The house is so huge I only use a minute part myself, so I thought, why not change it into a guest house? I can even imagine myself later in life enjoying the role of host to the guests," Manuel explains. The old manor house from the eighteenth century offers fabulous facilities for people who want to relax. From next season, a manager couple will be hired to run the country house hotel.

On the ground floor of the manor house are guest areas like the kitchen, living room, games room, reception, hall and bath-rooms. The first floor has two suites, one of them with a library, two big lounges and bathrooms, all decorated with period furni-ture. The second floor comprises four suites for the guests, and is also decorated with antique furniture. A large swimming pool is mainly heated by 34 solar panels. In the pool house, the guests can find a bar, bathrooms, Turkish baths and rest rooms.

In the courtyard is a huge stable complex for Manuel da Silva's horses; breeding horses is another of his passions. Guests will be able to use them both for riding and carriage driving - except perhaps for that rare, wonderful gem, his white Lipizzaner horse.

"At weekends I try to come to Quinta de Aldeia as often as possible. In winter, I very much look forward to the hunting season. Being on horseback, riding with 40-50 other hunters, with the hounds barking - the speed, the hunt, that's a real adrenalin kick!"

Choosing
the home

Choosing the home

Europe is growing. Not in terms of the population but of the expanding economy of the first decade of the new millennium. The last time Europe experienced a fast-expanding economy was in the 1960s and 1970s, when the suburban landscape was changed by a huge surge in the construction of new homes. The recent economic boom of the new millennium has had a similar effect: an increasing demand for more and better housing. The focus of these new homes is first and foremost on visions of daylight, space and openness to the landscape; but also on large kitchens, bigger rooms for children and more and better bathrooms.

More than 80% of all Europeans live in towns and cities, and the new housing developments are mainly in areas close to existing cities. Some people have chosen to live in one of the new housing estates, in terraced houses or in apartments constructed on the outskirts of cities all over the European continent. A few privileged Europeans have built a new home right out in the countryside, preferably with spectacular views and a sense of having the outside inside.

Many of the new generations of Europeans grew up in homes with roof windows in their own children's rooms, and thus acquired a different view of what a home should be like. To them, daylight coming through roof windows was not something to be added to a house as an afterthought. A loft room was not a dark, forlorn place or just a necessary construction to support a roof. To them, a loft room is an integral part of a home, giving the extra space and daylight that is so much in demand.

This chapter, 'Choosing the home', visits people who have chosen new imaginative homes, all permeated by daylight and opening up to the outdoors whether they are in the cool, humid climate of northern Europe or in a much warmer environment in the south. We visit newly constructed detached houses with spectacular views of the landscape on an island off the rocky Norwegian coast, in a tiny village in the Spanish Pyrenees, on the smiling southern coast of Sweden and in an open, child-friendly terraced housing estate in the densely populated Netherlands; but also gated and secured communities in the growing megalopolises Moscow and Istanbul; and finally, apartment blocks of innovative design in the Netherlands.

The plot of land in the middle of the countryside offered the possibility of siting a house with panoramic views towards the south, an important factor in a country as far north as Norway.

At no extra cost, Sabine Moshövel was able to change details in the design of the prefabricated Mira house, such as parts of the façade and having an open kitchen.

Northern lights and sea views: Mira House, Kolvereid, Nærøy, Norway

"I'll never forget the first night in my new house: lying in bed and looking through the roof windows at the magical northern lights flashing in green, yellow, pink and blue colours across the night sky," says Sabine Moshövel. A medical doctor, she moved to Norway from Germany to work as a GP in the small local district of Kolvereid with 5,000 inhabitants, 1,500 of which live in the small town where she has her clinic.

After a couple of years, Sabine decided to stay on longer in Norway, so she set out to buy a house of her own. At first she considered buying the house she rented, but that would mean a lot of renovation. She also wanted a place where she could better appreciate the magnificent Norwegian landscape in all its splendour from inside the house. So she decided to build a completely new, modern house.

The plot of land she finally bought was eleven kilometres outside town in the forest on a rocky promontory 40 m above sea level. The plot was suitable for building a house with panoramic views facing directly south, and a small hill behind would shelter it from the cold northern winds. A road had already been constructed and there were water and electricity supplies because

of a house farther up the road. "My new neighbours were really kind and welcoming. They enjoyed having somebody else living nearby – being a doctor I'm rather popular," Sabine smiles. "And they enjoy the fact that their water pressure has doubled since I moved in."

"Here in Norway it wasn't easy to find a modern prefabricated house that could have the amount of daylight inside that I wanted and the big, open views of the beautiful countryside. I had catalogues and leaflets sent from many builders, but none seemed quite right. Then, finally, I happened to see a drawing of a house called Mira in a VELUX brochure from a Norwegian builder who had been working with some fine architects, and it seemed to have everything I wanted. So I asked for some photos to learn more. Well, they had never built this model before, it was completely new! I imagined this house and my stunning views of the landscape would go really well together. At no extra cost, I was able to change details in the design of the house – like parts of the façade and having an open kitchen. The whole building process was very fast and efficient, everything came prefabricated.

"When the house was completed, it was even better than I had ever imagined. I've lived here for three years now and it's a daily joy," Sabine Moshövel smiles contentedly.

Bedrooms, bathrooms, sauna and workroom face north, but the sloping angle of the windows lets in more daylight than would otherwise be possible.

The whole southern façade opens up to the spectacular panoramic sea views of the Norwegian landscape. The daylight is enhanced by the many roof windows.

"My favourite place in the house – well, I don't have just one. In summertime, when it never gets dark, I enjoy the views of the surrounding nature; in the morning from the kitchen, in the evening from the sitting room. In wintertime when it's dark most of the time, my favourite place is in the sauna. It has a roof window and it is quite magical sitting in the sauna heat looking up at the snow falling on the windowpane."

"My free time is not always during weekends as I'm a doctor, but when I am free, I often have friends over. My house has lots of space and everybody loves coming here enjoying the fabulous nature views. I like the Norwegian Christmas traditions, last year we were a lot of friends here all baking and cooking and really enjoying the facilities of the open plan of the house."

Mountain retreat: Casa de los Pirineos Españoles, Das, Spain

The high, rugged mountain range of the Pyrenees is shared by Spain and France. Today the formerly desolate, sparsely populated region is a favourite with skiers, mountain climbers and walkers alike.

When Jordi Cubiñà decided to build his new house in the small village of Das in the Pyrenees, it was because of a lifelong love affair with the wild countryside with its high mountain ridges surrounding the village. Das is a tiny village of only 165 inhabitants, situated at a height of 1,200 m and surrounded by mountain peaks as high as 2,500 m, with easy access to Spanish, French and Andorran ski stations. A native of Barcelona, Jordi Cubiñà has loved skiing and hiking in the area ever since he was 10-12 years old and felt a strong attachment to this particular region of the Pyrenees. So when the opportunity arose to build a house in Das exactly to his liking, he was really tempted.

"The house attracted considerable attention during the two years it was being constructed in 2003-2004. This area is known for its traditional architecture with sloping roofs, large eaves, walls of natural local stone in dry masonry and slate floors, traditions we wanted to preserve in the house while adopting a mod-

102

"My favourite place in the house is the big living room and the kitchen. I appreciate the daylight and the beautiful, ever-changing mountain panorama."

The high, rugged mountain range the Pyrenees is shared by Spain and France. The region is a favourite with skiers, mountain climbers and hikers. This area is known for its traditional architecture with sloping roofs, large eaves, walls of natural local stone in dry masonry and slate floors, traditions Jordi Cubiñà wanted to preserve in the house while adopting a modern approach and design for the house itself.

ern approach and design for the house itself. After the completion of the house, the reactions are really positive," Jordi Cubiñà says. He owns four furniture shops in Barcelona, but spends as much time as possible in his mountain retreat.

The 'day zones' of the house face south with spectacular views of the surroundings. The living and dining areas open up onto the garden, the kitchen and the library. The parents' bedroom, dressing room and bathroom are in the west, with a guest room and two large children's rooms with a bathroom each in the east. The areas for parents and children/guests both open out to an interior courtyard that lets everyone enjoy the lovely view of the mountain panorama. One floor below, built into the sloping landscape, are the service areas – garage, heating and storage – as well as an apartment for the servants. From the sports room there is direct access to the swimming pool outside – the mountain retreat has more to offer than just skiing!

Despite the heavy natural materials of the house, it seems very light and open. The large panorama windows face south, as in the house in Norway, and here in Spain roof windows also provide for close contact with daylight and the surroundings.

"At weekends, I come here as often as possible. I enjoy the wild mountain area around here; I go hiking in summer and skiing in winter. The place is popular with my friends too, so often houseguests join me for a weekend."

Back to back: Hittarp, Helsingborg, Sweden

"Here the horizon is open and free," Carl-Gustaf Andersson says and inhales the fresh sea air from the beach at Hittarp, north of the town of Helsingborg in southern Sweden. He bought the plot of land right on the coast back in 1998 because of its unique position. Together with his neighbours, the Nielssons, he had seen possibilities in the plot of land with a small wooden summer cottage on the other side of the street. "We planned to build a double house allowing both families to have the beautiful view of the sea with the Danish coast of north Zealand on the other side."

"The sea view was the most important consideration," Carl-Gustaf Andersson says, "but there were other factors too: we wanted as much daylight as possible, and the building materials were to be of enduring quality and easy to maintain. Oak and the dark Brazilian wood were chosen, and all the floors are in dark Italian granite tiles both inside and outside to balance the white interior. And then it's easy to clean," he says with a smile.

To have both houses opening their façades to the sea view, they had to share a common wall, which meant no windows were possible there. They found an ingenious daylight solution by

An ingenious solution to the windowless common wall between the twin houses was found by placing roof windows along the ridges of the roof, letting daylight into the open-plan kitchen/living room. The ceilings go right up to the ridge beams, giving a height of four metres.

"We planned to build a double house giving both families the beautiful view of the sea with the Danish coast of northern Zealand on the other side."

The Andersson family has added a very special installation – a 1 m² glass plate hanging invisibly under the roof windows. "It produces an even better effect of light in the kitchen. Sometimes we put art on it, like this life-like babydoll, which gives rise to a lot of discussions among friends!"

placing roof windows in the twin roofs, letting daylight into the open-plan kitchen/living room with dramatic effects. The ceiling is open right up to the ridge beam, giving it a height of four metres. The roof windows are in pairs, creating a daylight effect much appreciated by Carl-Gustaf Andersson. "From an aesthetic point of view, the double pairs of windows are better, and they let twice as much daylight into our home, an important factor here in Sweden, especially during the winter months, when it's really grey and dark."

The Andersson family has added a very special installation – a 1 m² glass plate hanging invisibly under the roof windows. "It produces an even better effect of light in our kitchen. Sometimes we put art on it, which gives rise to a lot of discussions among our friends!"

Dash's father, Romeo Oemar, has come home early today from his job as an accountant in Rotterdam to be with his son, and is clearly enjoying the afternoon very much.

The Hageneiland Estate is built around small gardens and winding paths, creating new, peaceful, enjoyable views at every turn, very much as in a small village. All the cars must park outside; between the houses all traffic is pedestrian.

Child's play: Hageneiland, Ypenburg, Netherlands

The little boy is eagerly tugging his father's trousers: "Dash play!" he says firmly and looks admiringly at the older girl on the swing. His father has come home early today from his job as an accountant in Rotterdam to be with his son and is clearly enjoying the afternoon very much. The children's playground little Firdas wanted so much is surrounded by small gardens and winding paths, creating new, peaceful, enjoyable views at every turn, very much as in a small village. There is not a car in the area: between the houses all the traffic is pedestrian – except of course on bicycles. After all, we are in The Netherlands!

The colourful houses in the housing estate Hageneiland (meaning 'hedge island') look a little like children's building blocks. Their façades and roofs are similar with their clear, appealing colours – red, green, silver, blue and black – but they are all made of differently textured materials. The red is brick roof tiles, the black is wood shingles, the blue and green are flat polyurethane panels and the shiny, rippling grey is aluminium sheets. In a healthy mixture, some houses are rented, some are privately owned. They are detached or terraced houses, many with the option of extra rooms under the roof.

Dash, almost two yeas old, lives in a green house with his father Romeo and his mother Zanaida, who is an officer in the Rotterdam Police Force. The Oemars bought the house in Hageneiland three years ago when they were expecting Firdas. "We wanted to live in a place that was really good for a child. The house has a big, closed yard for him to play in now. Here in Hageneiland it's really safe, so when Dash is older he can go and play with other children by himself," Romeo explains. "We also had to look for a price we could afford as first-time buyers, and since I came from Amsterdam and Zanaida from Rotterdam we also looked for a house in between the two. We chose this new house here on the hedge island because it matched all of our wishes."

The Hageneiland is just one small housing estate of 119 homes among many other estates built on the grounds of a former military airport. The whole new housing area now contains 15,000 homes. Hageneiland's colourful village atmosphere stands out clearly from the many traditional terraced housing estates around it.

"Most people here have chosen to live in Hageneiland because they are young families with children, just as we are," Romeo Oemar explains, while Firdas clearly signals that he wants to play with his Dad – now!

"We wanted to live in a place that was really good for a child. The house has a big, closed yard for Firdas to play in. Here in Hageneiland it's really safe, so when Dash is older he can go and play with other children by himself," Romeo explains. "We also had to look for a price we could afford as first-time buyers."

The colourful houses in the housing estate Hageneiland (meaning 'hedge island') look a little like children's building blocks.

"My favourite place in the house is the big living room. Here we can be with our son Dash and he can play everywhere. And also I like to relax with the television here."

"At weekends, we go shopping and do chores. We also visit our families, who live in Amsterdam and Rotterdam. Before we had Dash, we often visited friends and went to the cinema. Now it's much more about being a family."

Intelligent luxury in the dacha: Korovino, Krasnogorsky, Moscow, Russia

One of the frequent descriptions of the nearby, former princely palace of Arkhangelskoe is 'a corner of paradise', a designation the new village of Korovino also means to earn. Arkhangelskoe Palace is today a much-loved visitors' attraction with an impressive art collection and a huge, beautiful Italianate park.

Moscow is not only the capital of Russia, it is also the second largest city in Europe with more than ten million inhabitants registered, plus an unknown number of unregistered ones; its metropolitan area ranks among the largest urban areas in the world. So the 'outskirts' of Moscow often means something quite a distance from the centre. But despite its country-like appearance, the Krasnogorsky district of the Moscow region is only 20 km west of the capital. Here we find Korovino, a newly built housing estate.

Moscow was recently designated the most expensive city in the world to live in, and Korovino Village caters to an increasingly large middle-class group with wealth generated by the expanding Russian economy, which throughout the first decade of the new millennium has generated growth figures of around 7% a year.

Traditionally, the inhabitants of Moscow have always loved the idea of having a 'dacha' in a village in the countryside, outside the city; the dacha is usually a small wooden cabin on a plot of land just big enough to grow some fresh vegetables. By calling itself a 'village', Korovino evokes the romance of the past, but this village is rather different: the new cottages vary in size between 287

Colourful Russian dream bathroom with lots of daylight.

The new 'cottages' in Korovino vary in area between 287 and 380 m². The 144 blocks of terraced or semi-detached houses are placed in small groups in large, green spaces with well-kept lawns and trees.

and 380 m². The 144 blocks of terraced or semi-detached houses are in small groups in large, green spaces with well-kept lawns and trees.

Young people living in Moscow want many of the same things in life as most other young people in Europe: fresh air, green and pleasant surroundings, quiet, space for the children, a safe environment, nature. In Korovino Village all this is on offer along with an emphasis on security, a factor that is extra important to the new inhabitants; the place calls itself an 'intelligent village'. Every house in the village can be connected to the central security system. Cameras installed in the home to look after the children are an option too. The IT systems also provide surveillance of the house for the owners when they are away from home for any length of time. Since many young Russians go on holiday a lot, this is also a feature that is increasingly in demand.

The surrounding landscape contains forests, lakes and moors and the air of luxury living given by the historic Arkhangelskoe Palace near Korovino, today a much-loved visitors' attraction with an impressive art collection and a huge, beautiful Italianate park. At the end of the 1700s, the country estate Arkhangelskoe was the most lavish, indulgent and celebrated playground of Moscow's wealthy aristocracy. The estate was owned by Prince Nikolai Yusupov, one of the richest men in the country, who not only took to art collecting and science, but corresponded with the French philosopher Voltaire, discussed poetry with Russia's favourite writer Pushkin, spent a fortune on this wonderful country estate, and according to historical gossip even kept a harem of beautiful women there for his pleasure! One of the frequent descriptions of the Arkhangelskoe Palace Estate is 'a corner of paradise', a designation the new village of Korovino also means to earn.

"Our favourite place in the house is the patio. It is filled with daylight all year round and we enjoy the feeling of being outside in the garden when we are inside."

"At weekends, we have friends over for lunch at least twice a month, we light the barbecue and make different salads, the children play around and we just enjoy life."

The Carpe Diem estate has a lot of space: 87% of the grounds are green areas. It offers many facilities like a tennis court and a large swimming pool. The families feel safe letting the children play on their own because the estate has security cameras everywhere with direct links to the houses so parents can always check on their TV screens what their children are doing.

Country living in a megalopolis: Carpe Diem, Çekmeköy, Istanbul, Turkey

Istanbul competes with Moscow as the most populous city in Europe. According to official statistics, Istanbul has a population of eleven million, but like in Moscow there is also a large number of unregistered residents.

For several years the Turkish economy has been experiencing a boom with an average annual growth rate of 7.5%, and one consequence of this has been a huge demand for new and better houses from many prosperous young families. Like the fast-growing economy of Russia, Istanbul, the ancient, beautiful and fascinating capital on both sides of the Bosphorus, keeps expanding its outskirts. The growth is less and less in the form of the densely-packed high-rise apartment blocks of former times, but increasingly in the form of new, gated communities of terraced or detached houses, each boasting its own garden and parking space for the cars that are necessary to commute to work in the city, and offering shared facilities like swimming pools and tennis courts. In each new living area, security is a high priority, just as it is in Moscow. The former village of Çekmeköy, 25 km outside Istanbul on the Asian side, is currently one of the most attractive places to live.

120

In Turkey the dream of a 'yala' (country home) in a cool, green 'köyu' (village) is high on the list of priorities for many families with children, and this dream of green meadows, country living and the stability of the small town is busily promoted by the Cekmeköy municipality. The former village is still surrounded by lush green pine forests covering gentle, rolling hills. Gated housing estates are sprouting up all around, and as an ironic result the attractive forest is shrinking by the day.

"The air pollution in Istanbul was not good for our daughters, and the traffic congestion in the centre is indescribable. Summers can be very hot, and here in Cekmeköy it's at least a couple of degrees cooler," Attila Sever explains. An engineer in an industrial export business, he moved into the Carpe Diem estate with his wife Nurhan and their two daughters two years ago when the project was completed. "We didn't move because of a lack of space, since we lived in an apartment of 400 m² on the top two floors of a building; we chose to move here to Cekmeköy because of the fresh air and the green forest close by."

"All 26 families living here in the Carpe Diem estate have children, so there's always somebody to play with," Nurhan Sever explains. "There is a lot of space here – 87% of the grounds are green areas. We have many facilities, a tennis court just behind our house and a great swimming pool. We feel safe letting the children play on their own because the estate has security cameras everywhere with direct links to our house so we can always check on our TV screens what the children are doing."

"But the others of my age are just boys. No girls, it's just so annoying," 11-year-old Dilara says in very good English. "I wish I had some girlfriends here!" "She plays football all the time," Attila Sever says proudly, "and the other fathers say that she is the best of the bunch!" Like her 15-year-old sister, Dilara goes to a school where all lessons are in English. "Well, my big sister left school last year and now she's attending a French college and will leave that with a university entrance exam in French. I want to do that too."

Like her husband, Nurhan is an engineer; her degree is in industrial engineering, her husband's in electronics. "My wife worked as an engineer for 14 years, but as the educational system here in Turkey is very competitive, she gave up working to help

"I select the seeds from the best and sweetest tomatoes when I eat them and then start new plants. I have the nursery plants in the daylight under the roof windows on the top floor with the sunscreen, and as they grow I select the strongest ones and put them in the garden. But I don't do the practical work of gardening; Carpe Diem has a crew of gardeners who do what we ask in our private gardens – that is included in the fees for the estate."

Dilara, 11, goes to an English school like her sister earlier.

Each house in the Carpe Diem estate is about 450 m² in area on four floors plus patios and balconies.

The former village of Cekmeköy is still surrounded by lush green pine forests covering gentle, rolling hills. Gated housing estates are sprouting up everywhere around, and as a result the attractive forest is shrinking by the day.

The shared house by the swimming pool offers facilities to the house-owners like games, a huge TV screen mainly used for watching football together, and a café with a housekeeper.

Most of the Severs' family time is spent on the glass-covered patio; they feel it is like being out in the garden full of flowers and fruit trees. The patio has a radiant heating system for the winters, when Istanbul can get really cold.

our girls with their schoolwork. I'm away a lot in my job, so it was really necessary."

The houses of the Carpe Diem estate are each about 450 m² in area, in four floors plus patios and balconies. Most of the family time is spent on the glass-covered patio where it feels like being out in the garden full of flowers and fruit trees. The patio has a radiant heating system for the winters, when Istanbul can get really cold. "Last winter we had minus 6°C and all my orange trees just died," Attila Sever sighs. "I'm passionate about plants!" In a corner of the garden he grows cucumbers, peppers and tomatoes of pink, yellow and classic red varieties. "I select the seeds from tomatoes when I eat them and then I start new plants. I have the nursery plants in the daylight under the roof windows on the top floor, and as they grow I select the strongest ones and put them in the garden. But I don't do the practical work of gardening; Carpe Diem has a crew of gardeners who do what we ask them in our private gardens – that is included in the fees for the estate. We just pay for the plants and get the very best ones that way." Attila Sever's passion for plants has made him expand the hobby into a new venture. "With some friends I've started an experiment to produce cherries of a sort that is twice the size of ordinary cherries, like plums. They're so tasty and sweet. We've bought virgin land in the woods near Izmir in the Aegean part of Turkey and expect to harvest 800 tonnes for export next year."

Walking through the grounds of the estate, it is evident that the veranda patios are favourite places for many residents. Nurhan waves to her neighbour, who is working at her computer; as an independent consultant, she also enjoys the contact with the neighbours.

"Our eldest daughter of 15 has begun complaining of being so far away from the city centre. As a teenager she finds this place boring," Attila Sever smiles, "but we just love living here!"

Choosing city life: The Armada, Paleiskwartier, s'Hertogenbosch, Netherlands

The number of city-dwellers in Europe just keeps growing, and as a consequence most towns and cities encourage construction of new attractive housing projects within their central areas to meet the increasing demand for city living. The design of the new projects often takes the form of tower block apartments with huge glass windows and large terraces inviting the outside inside. The new apartments are frequently built on areas lying as wasteland close to the inner cities; i.e. old abandoned industrial areas, railway areas and harbours.

These new areas for city living are especially attractive to two major groups: the younger generation living as singles or in couples, and the more senior group who wants to choose a different kind of home for when their children move away. Both groups have the same wish to enjoy the facilities and culture offered by the city centres.

A good example of this new city living can be found in the Dutch city of s'Hertogenbosch in the southern part of the country. The Netherlands is one of the most densely populated areas of Europe. In s'Hertogenbosch the city council planned to use a huge, deserted railway area next to the very old city centre. When finished, the area was to have a theatre, a museum, a conference centre, shopping facilities and a whole new city neighbourhood of apartment buildings. One sector of the new Paleiskwartier ('Palace Quarter') stands out from all the others with their more traditional apartment buildings: the ten houses called 'The Armada' (because that is what they look like). The houses are built to maximise daylight in every apartment and to incorporate environment-friendly energy systems. In 2004 the 'Armada' residential development in s'Hertogenbosch was given the 'Best Loved Building' award by the Society of Architects in the Netherlands.

The ten houses are called 'The Armada' because they look a little like a fleet of sailing ships. The houses are built to maximise the light in every apartment and to incorporate environment-friendly energy systems. In 2004 the 'Armada' residential development in s'Hertogenbosch was given the 'Best Loved Building' award by the Society of Architects in the Netherlands.

Jorinde and André van der Veer enjoy the southern patio, almost an extension of their light-filled living room.

Colours and light for the whole family

"It was mainly our teenage son who convinced us to buy these apartments," says André van der Veer, who lives with his wife Jorinde and their teenage daughter and son in two adjacent but very different apartments of almost 200 m² each. Like the families in Slovenia and in Paris visited earlier, this Dutch family has created a solution so they can appreciate living together with their teenage children while both the parents and their children can pursue their own interests.

"The real estate company I owned three years ago was responsible for the sale of the apartments in the Armada," André van der Veer explains, "and when we had an 'Open House' for potential customers, the whole family was involved. Our son Matthijs helped by taking care of the open house in two of the large 7th-floor apartments at the top of the building. He liked the prospect of being so close to the city centre, to his school and his friends, and he really enjoyed the layout and the light-filled surround-

ings. And so he convinced us," André says with a big contented smile.

For many years the van der Veers had lived in the countryside in a huge, dark old farmhouse on an estate with a swimming pool and lots of facilities for the children. Like most families with young children, they had chosen to live in a green, child-friendly, safe environment. But as the children grew into teenagers, they chose the city rather than the countryside chosen by their parents.

"We were able to change the layout of the apartments such that the two are connected by a door inside the apartments. We live in one, and Matthijs and Roosje, aged 17 and 19, have their rooms in the other apartment, where I also have a completely separate office with its own entrance," André says. "I sold my real estate business last year and have chosen to work just a few days. I do consultancy for public housing organisations and the Government on questions relating to housing policy. After an illness, my wife and I decided that we wanted to concentrate on the fam-

Matthijs, 17, studies computers. He was the initiator of the family's move to the apartments in the Armada.

"My favourite place in the house is the big living room and the south terrace. The light here is really lovely. Sitting in the sunlight on the terrace with a good book, that's what I like too."
"My favourite place is my office. I've started studying law after my retirement, just out of interest, so I enjoy it; here it's so quiet and peaceful."

"At weekends, we are together with our family and friends a lot. We have a total of five children and so far five grandchildren. We like eating and drinking together."

128

ily and enjoy life together, so we now spend a lot of time travelling in Europe in our camper, which even has a small scooter on the back so we can get around cities easily."

The large living room is always suffused with daylight whatever the weather. On the southern side, it opens up through huge windows to a large patio with flowerpots and plenty of room for a dining table and comfortable chairs. On the northern side, glass doors open to a glass-covered winter-garden terrace. The room gets even more daylight from several windows in the corners.

The rounded roof of the building leaves space for a cosy smaller room with roof windows, where the family has made a television room to relax in. The bedroom also has a rounded wall, where two roof windows give a view of the stars from the bed.

Everywhere in the apartments, colourful art mirrors the vitality and energy of the family. Some pieces have been created by artistic family members, others by artists exhibiting in the real estate company André van der Veer used to own. "We have always liked art, and bought a lot of things we liked." Jorinde van der Veer enjoys making pottery, and the huge apartment even has room for a potter's workroom and a small kiln. Roosje studies at the design academy and plays the piano seriously, so she has a baby grand in the apartment that she shares with her brother. His interest – and his subject of study – is information technology, so he has a huge amount of information technology gadgets on his large working table.

"Even though the inspiration to buy the apartments came from Matthijs, we really love living here! In our old house it was always so dark; we had to have the electric light on even in the daytime. Here it's always light. It's also great to be close to the city centre. We just cross the railway by the bridge at the station and we are there. And it's so easy to go to Amsterdam by train; we never take the car because of the traffic congestion here in Holland."

Roosje, 19, shares the apartment adjacent to her parents with her brother.

A safe haven

"My husband loved sitting in the sun on our beautiful sunny patio. That's where he spent most of his time in the last period of his life," Riekie van de Wetering says. "We had planned to enjoy life together in our new apartment, but we only had a year and a half together here." The terrace is filled with flowers in pots, almost as in a garden. "Now, when I'm on the terrace, I think so much about him. It's only a few months since he passed away." A big black-and-white cat takes possession of one of the comfortable chairs on the patio with a demeanour that clearly indicates he owns it.

"We very much enjoyed the fact that we could change the standard layout of the apartment of 185 m². For example, I really wanted to have a big bathroom, so we took some space from the guest room, which is small now, but that's OK."

Before moving to the new apartment in the Armada, Riekie van de Wetering and her husband lived eight kilometres outside s'Hertogenbosch in a house with a big garden in the middle of the woods. "The garden is the only thing I miss, that's why I've tried to make a garden on both patios."

"I love living here and feel very safe. There are always neighbours around. I'm very close to my job in the local authority. I just walk across the footbridge at the station and I'm right in the centre of the city. And when I go out in the city with my friends in the evening, I feel safe walking home alone. It's really like living in the city but without the noise."

"My favourite place in the house is my office next to the living room. I like the intimacy of the room when I work under the VELUX window. I do a lot of my work from my home. The saxophone and the guitar in the window to the terrace were my husband's. He didn't really play very well, but he just enjoyed it so much!"

"At weekends, I like bicycling in the countryside. If the weather is bad – and that's quite often the case here in Holland – I go with friends to enjoy the city, or I just stay at home reading a good book."

Lighting up
the city loft

Living under the old roofs was a cold, draughty experience and you only did so out of necessity.

'The Poor Poet', a popular painting by the German artist Carl Spitzweg from 1839, vividly depicts what living in the attic meant in former times.

Lighting up the city loft

Living in an attic in the centre of a European city is regarded as the height of attractiveness today. If an apartment for sale is described as 'attic', 'penthouse', 'loft living', 'New York atmosphere' or similar code words, you can be sure the price is top-end – especially if an apartment has the added charm of opening up to the outside by way of a balcony, a hidden patio, or best of all, a complete roof deck.

However, the attractiveness of attic living in a city is of very recent date. The attic space in cities used to be the opposite of attractive: a place where no one lived voluntarily. Usually it was a dark, cold or scorching hot place where only the poor, the servants, the poets and the painters lived – out of necessity. And yet this space, the humble attic, has provided inspiration for many European artists' much loved stories and dramas.

The fairytale writer Hans Christian Andersen used the setting of the attic to emphasise the destitution in his story of a poor street child, 'The Little Match-Girl'.

"Shivering with cold and hunger, she crept along; poor little child, she looked the picture of misery. She had drawn her little feet under her, but she could not keep off the cold; and she dared not go home, for she had sold no matches, and could not take home even a penny of money. Her father would certainly beat her; besides, it was almost as cold at home as here, for they had only the roof to cover them, through which the wind howled, although the largest holes had been stopped with straw and rags."

In Puccini's very popular opera La Bohème, a central scene is the first meeting of the two lovers. It takes place in a cold, dark attic in Paris where the students use their last chair as wood for the stove to have at least some warmth for a short while. The student Rudolpho and the seamstress Mimi stumble upon each other under the roof of the dark attic, unable to see because the draught in the attic has blown out both their candles. Nevertheless they fall madly in love as he romantically sings the song *"Che gelida manina"* ... *"How cold your little hand is, let me warm it in mine"*.

Oliver Twist by Charles Dickens is another story so beloved by generations of Europeans that, since the invention of the movie industry and later of the TV medium, each generation has made its own film or television version. In the dramatic story, a gang of boys lives in the attic owned by the villain Fagin:

"The walls and ceiling of the room were perfectly black with age and dirt. There was a deal table before the fire ... several rough beds made of old sacks were huddled side by side on the floor. Seated round the table were four or five boys, none older than the Dodger, smoking long clay pipes, and drinking spirits with the air of middle-aged men. These all crowded about their associate as he whispered a few words to the Jew; and then turned round and grinned at Oliver. So did the Jew himself, toasting-fork in hand. "This is him, Fagin," said Jack Dawkins; "my friend Oliver Twist.""

The attic may have been the space of myths, of stories and of romances for a very long time, but in real life its undesirability lasted right up to the end of the 20th century. And then it was almost like an explosion: from the beginning of the 1990s, a new generation of Europeans began returning to the old city centres. Daring artists were some of the first to take a look at deserted warehouses by the waterways or dark, hidden lofts, and to see possibilities in their strong structures for creating fabulous homes. Butcher districts, workers' tenements, historic heritage houses, all were viewed with new eyes.

Increasingly, people wanted to live in the city centres. The young did not automatically move out of the cities when they started families. Middle-aged couples sold suburban homes to be close to the many cultural opportunities of the city. 'Loft living' became the hottest, most desirable trend. The scarcity of available space for living in the city centres kick-started innovative solutions: old dusty attics of city houses, long used just for junk, as even students and artists had moved out, now found new functions as settings for chic loft living.

One of the major prerequisites for this magical change was the possibility of letting in daylight, a feature so amply afforded by roof windows. Architects as well as private citizens realised new ways of letting in the magic of daylight, creating bright, airy apartments – preferably opening up to the outside via new roof terraces or bright, VELUX enabled balconies.

This chapter, 'Lighting up the city loft', visits contemporary city lofts in some of the newly-transformed spaces of old city centres in Europe. Some people have taken on the challenge of converting an attic in a protected historic area like the Castle Hill district

A maid's room in the attic – now a museum exhibit.

in Budapest; some have turned undesirable features from the past into settings for contemporary living, like the former bomb shelter in Cologne. Others have changed nondescript loft areas in Copenhagen and Milan into spacious contemporary homes; others again have gone for better insulation and eco-friendly solutions in Vienna. An artist enjoys her view over the roofs of Paris, and in Madrid and in Sofia, two young architect couples have quite independently of each other changed an old artist's studio into open spaces with lots of daylight.

Space and light in a city loft: Salamancar, Madrid, Spain

The lowest parts of the apartment have become bedroom and working space, all in open plan with the rest of the apartment.

When two young Spanish architects, Gálata Sáenz and Juan Carnicero, finished university in 2001, they went hunting for a place to live. They were most interested in one in the very centre of Madrid, the dynamic, beautiful capital of Spain. And they wanted it to have daylight and outdoor space, features not easily found in the historic centre, especially on a limited budget.

Searching for a place they could change into their own personally designed home, they happened to look at a painter's old attic in a central part of Madrid called Salamancar. Apart from a skylight, the attic was dark, with many small partitions and a very low ceiling. It was scorching hot in summer and chilly and draughty in winter.

But the young couple saw something behind this dark maze that concealed the possibilities of the place. They bought the attic and started a complete transformation.

First of all, they removed all the partition walls, leaving an open U-shaped area of 140 m². The only door installed afterwards leads to the bathroom facilities.

Then they took down the low ceiling, opening the attic up all the way to the central rafters, giving them a height of 4.2 m in

A major obstacle to creating a light-filled, airy home in the old attic was the low rafters, a feature typical of roof constructions with low pitches. The young architects found an ingenious solution: instead of the wooden rafters, they installed transverse steel wires that gave them a well-lit, spacious room.

140

Right in the old centre of Madrid, Gálata and Juan were able to construct a fabulous terrace opening up from the living zone of the apartment.

the living room. The parts of the apartment with a lower height were designated as bedroom and study area.

A major obstacle to creating a light-filled, airy home in the old attic was the low height of the rafters, a feature typical of roof constructions with low pitches. The young architects found an ingenious solution: instead of the wooden rafters, they installed transverse steel wires that gave them a well-lit, spacious room construction.

Gálata and Juan were able to construct an enchanting terrace opening up from the living zone of the apartment. However, even together with three ordinary windows this did not provide enough daylight in the formerly dark attic. Wanting natural light to permeate the whole apartment, they installed roof windows all along the ridge beams of the U-shaped apartment. The effect of the changing daylight on the bright white interior, the golden wood of the floors and the classically simple modern style is striking.

"Our favourite place in the apartment... well, we actually have two: the living room and the terrace, because they are both multi-functional spaces with beautiful views."

"On Sundays, we like to have breakfast on the terrace and go playing with our children in the 'Retiro' park."

The whole roof structure was taken down and a new one was constructed, incorporating a row of roof windows.

Heritage challenges: Castle Hill, Budapest, Hungary

'Varhegy', the Castle Hill and the Castle District of Budapest, is a designated UNESCO World Heritage Site. This entire part of the city is so well preserved that when the film about Mozart was made, the place they found that looked most like an 18th-century Central European city was right there. Not only interesting buildings, streets and squares, but also the former royal palace, three churches, six museums, and fortresses and bastions greet the many visitors.

This kind of magnificent heritage certainly poses a challenge if you want to change a house. The owner of a large house on the Danube side of the hill planned to convert his attic space into two large luxury apartments, so he asked a famous architect to undertake the task.

The whole roof structure was taken down and a new one was constructed. During this work the house revealed several surprises and secrets, and many unknown, hidden air shafts and chimneys appeared where there should be none. The air shafts were re-used in various ways; one of them was enlarged and now serves as a small green interior courtyard, transformed into an interior space by a glass wall on the living room/dining room

side. The body of the house is solid, which means that several parts of the interior had no daylight at all. So all along the centre of the ceiling area, a long row of roof windows now opens up this formerly dark interior section of the apartment to delightful, ever-changing patterns of daylight.

The residents of the two apartments now have the privilege of living in extraordinary modern comfort in an extraordinary old city.

All along the centre of the ceiling area, a row of roof windows now opens up this formerly dark interior section of the apartment to delightful, ever-changing patterns of daylight.

Many unknown, hidden air shafts and chimneys appeared during the reconstruction process. The air shafts were re-used in various ways; one of them was enlarged and now serves as a small green interior courtyard, transformed into an interior space by a glass wall.

The heavy burden of history: Bomb shelter house, Nippes, Cologne, Germany

History has left its traces throughout the cities of Europe. Some buildings have been declared historic heritage, while other parts of European history have left a legacy no one really wants to see. For example, what is to be done with the huge concrete bomb shelters from the Second World War?

In the quiet and neat neighbourhood of Nippes near the German town of Cologne, a bomb shelter 45 m long, 15 m deep and 7.5 m tall remained as a sad reminder of World War II. Vandalised by graffiti, heavy and silent, with no openings in its solid walls, the shelter had become a 'white spot' on the mental map of the neighbourhood. The citizens simply did not see it any more.

They do now. Some years ago, a young entrepreneur bought the shelter and held a competition, inviting proposals to make it habitable.

When you pass by in the street today, no trace of any bomb shelter is discernible. And yet it is there, incorporated into the new, airy, light-filled complex. In the new barrel-shaped roof of the former shelter, roof windows have been integrated, bringing daylight into the apartments from above.

When you enter the apartment of one of the new residents,

"My favourite place is the large couch in the two-storey living room that opens up towards the sky. It's just so light-filled, even on a gloomy day. From there I have a great view of the garden or my mahogany piano, which I inherited from my grand mother. I have a great passion for music."

Christoph, the first impression is of strong daylight, despite the fact that it is in the middle of the former shelter.

The walls are actually still solid, reinforced concrete, 1.10 m thick. In this apartment, the impressive wall cuts made to open up the shelter have been left unplastered, with the marks made by the diamond saw used to carve out the light sources on full display. Other owners have gone for a more serene, clean look by having everything covered with plaster and painted white.

One effect of the solid walls on the indoor climate is rather surprising. Because the large openings face west, the emphasis is on heat, not coolness. Assisted by the roof openings of the windows, the daylight also brings in radiant heat, warming the solid walls slowly but effectively. Normally this causes no problems, but on very hot summer days, Christoph has experienced a peculiar thing.

"We sat outside all evening, and when we finally decided to go inside, the apartment had become quite warm, so we opened the large sliding doors to let in the cool night air. After ten minutes the temperature had dropped and we closed the doors again. Within another five minutes, though, we had to open them all again – the massive concrete walls and decks had absorbed so much heat that they kept the whole apartment warm until next morning!"

"On Sundays, I prefer to stay in bed. My bedroom on the first floor is right next to the living room and also bathed in daylight."

152

"On Sundays, we like to go to the countryside. Even though we live in a big city with all the comforts and services we need, we love to get in touch with nature."

The anonymity of the house permitted a much more original reconstruction plan than could be used for more historically interesting, protected houses.

Green oasis in the city of fashion: Milan, Lombardy, Italy

Milan, the Italian capital of fashion and furniture, is a vibrant contemporary city with century upon century of treasures to be enjoyed, like the majestic Gothic cathedral.

When you live in Italy, the beauty of the historic heritage is evident at every turn. Milan, the capital of fashion and furniture, is a vibrant contemporary city with century upon century of treasures to be enjoyed – the majestic Gothic cathedral, the mystical Leonardo da Vinci fresco of The Last Supper, or the brilliant Art Nouveau glass galleries for the palaces of high fashion.

But even in Milan, you find very ordinary houses, places that are never really noticed. This ordinariness was turned to great advantage when the Lombardy region passed a law in 1997 encouraging the use of attics for living in. The anonymity of the houses permitted a much more original conversion plan than could be used in more historically interesting, protected houses, a fact that appealed greatly to the architect Francesco Florulli and his wife, who wanted to create their own home right in the vibrant city centre.

In Milan, houses from the 1900s often have penthouses on top of the original house, but this house had an ordinary, traditional low pyramidal roof that did not appear to leave much room for living space.

The creative solution of Francesco Florulli was to 'excavate' a

154

"My favourite room is the living room. Here I can relax when I get back from work, reading a book or magazine. During the summer the plants growing all around the appartment offer pleasant shading, protecting from sunlight and heat, providing at the same time some privacy. During the winter, when the plants are bare, the house has a fine view over Milan, providing a sensation of freedom and wideness."

156

During the hot summer, the cool green shade of the oasis filters the sunlight. In wintertime the lower sunbeams come through the many roof windows, which means savings on the heating budget. And in this 'house-on-a-house', even on the grey winter days of Milan, the rooms are filled with daylight.

roof terrace all around the central pyramid. The original roof was removed and a new, lighter structure constructed. All around the perimeter of the penthouse, new glass walls in a veranda-like construction completely opened up the apartment to the exterior.

Even though Milan is in the northern part of Italy, the summer season can still be very hot; so to avoid creating an unbearable hothouse, a green oasis was created instead. The wrap-around roof terrace was covered with wooden flooring, and underneath a waterproof membrane all rainwater is conducted to the bamboo hedges planted along the outer perimeter.

Together with semitransparent sunscreens on the upper roof windows, this is so effective that the owners chose not to have air conditioning installed. Instead, during the hot summer, the cool green shade of their oasis filters the sunlight. In the wintertime the lower sunbeams come through the many roof windows, and this means savings on the heating budget. And in this 'house-on-a-house', even on the grey winter days of Milan, the rooms are filled with daylight.

"My favourite place in our home is the kitchen. In the morning I enjoy my espresso coffee here while watching the sunrise and in the evening I enjoy the sunset, just by turning my head."

Self-made is well-made: Amager, Copenhagen, Denmark

The island of Amager east of Copenhagen is separated from the city by a narrow waterway. In the past, Central Copenhagen has always looked upon its close neighbour with disdain. Over there were wastelands with peasants farming for the city; and over there the city could conveniently dump all its refuse. As factories were built close to the bridges at the beginning of the twentieth century, neighbourhoods of five-storey red-brick apartment blocks were very soon built on Amager for the many new workers needed. Often these apartment buildings were organised as cooperative apartments, an ownership type that still exists.

Today a new young generation has discovered the rough charm and attractions of the old workers' neighbourhood. Amagerbrogade with its busy traffic is the old main artery, where Klaus Malmgren, a young carpenter, has converted a former fifth-floor clothes-drying loft along with a fourth-floor apartment into a fabulous, light-filled 260 m² home. When the property had to have a new roof, Klaus got the chance of exchanging his second-floor apartment for a fourth-floor apartment just below the enormous old loft used for storing the flotsam and jetsam of a century. He succeeded in convincing the cooperative to let

Klaus Malmgren, a young carpenter, has converted the fifth floor, a dark, dusty loft, along with a fourth-floor apartment, into a fabulous, light-filled 260 m² home. And he has made the whole conversion himself after working hours.

"On summer sundays, I like to chill out on my big terrace. The large glass doors make the outside feel like inside."

Amager Strandpark is only 1.5 km away from the busy street. Here Klaus can roller skate with his daughter Olivia for kilometres on smooth tracks in the dunes, enjoying fresh sea views towards Sweden, the tall windmills in the sea and a colourful spectacle of the kite surfers.

160

him buy the loft and started on the Sisyphus task of clearing out four and a half tonnes of debris, including seven iron stoves and truckloads of old furniture.

At first, all the building material was hoisted up by crane, but in the later phase it had to be carried manually up the stairs by Klaus and his friends. The permit to load and unload was restricted to between one and five in the morning, so the neighbours got very fed up with having their night sleep disturbed.

Today the former drying loft is where Klaus and his daughter Olivia spend most of their time at home. It has 16 m long solid mahogany floors, a height of 5.5 m to the central rafters, with 24 roof windows letting in daylight.

During the whole renovation process, Klaus worked constructing sets for film studios, so all the work on his own home had to be done in his spare time. The renovation took two and a half years – during which he also found time to work on a television makeover programme changing ugly homes into beautiful dream places. He just loves his job!

"My favourite place is the living room. It is our room; the rest of the apartment is filled with the children. I like watching television on our new big flatscreen."

"At weekends, we are usually in our datcha outside town. Mainly to relax but we also grow vegetables like tomatoes and cucumbers. In the autumn we very much enjoy gathering wild mushrooms in the vast woods surrounding St. Petersburg. In winter we mainly just stay at home."

The apartment blocks in Torjkovskaya Street are in a green area not far from the centre by metro. The other old blocks of apartments still have their leaky, uninsulated flat roofs.

Raising the roof: Torjkovskaya, St. Petersburg, Russia

St. Petersburg on the Baltic Sea, the former capital of imperial Russia, has a colourful gem of a city centre, all built in the 1700s with a complex of green leafy avenues and canals. However, now that the city has five million residents, huge new city neighbourhoods have been built, many of them in the 1950s in the communist era. The focus then was on utility and cheap housing, so none of the beauty of the centre is to be seen in the suburbs. Instead what meets the eye is innumerable identical concrete highrise blocks with flat roofs and no insulation

Not very far from the attractive centre, on Torjkovskaya Street, we find a five-storey 'Khrushchev building' where a completely new floor has been built on top of the existing flat-roofed building with careful consideration for the placement of roof windows to allow the loft apartments plenty of daylight in every room and a pleasant view of the surroundings. Apart from the much-needed renovation of the building, the aim was also to build equally necessary new apartments that were affordable to ordinary people.

The owners of the building had insufficient funding for repairs of the old leaky roof, so they decided to raise the roof by

Nina Sharipina loves the light from the roof window when she is washing up in her kitchen.

162

Sergei Valentinovich Sharipin has worked in the Navy all his life, and the family's interest in the sea is apparent everywhere in the apartment.

adding a storey of new attic apartments on the flat roof. The renovation also included insulation, thermostats on radiators and a new central heating system, all paid for by the addition of the new apartments on the roof.

The Sharipin family lives in one of these three-room attic apartments. "We waited for twelve years for this apartment, which we rent," Nina Mikhailovna Sharipina explains. "My husband Sergei works in the Navy and for many years we were stationed in the Baltic countries. But after the political changes and the independence of those countries, we had to return to St. Petersburg with the rest of the armed forces. It was difficult to find a place to live."

"Now we enjoy this green area and its closeness to the city centre – by metro it's only three stops to the Nevsky Prospect, the lovely main promenade and shopping street. We have lived here for five years now."

"The apartment is unusual, quite different from the traditional apartment concept where the attic is not a place for living," Nina explains. "Our visitors are often pleasantly and positively surprised by the green environment and the design of the apartment. Everything is really outstanding." The apartment has a terrace too, but it is closed off and, like all other Russians in St. Petersburg, the family does not use it. The lack of interest in indoor/outdoor living is one difference between Russians and other Europeans in the way they want to live.

Sergei Valentinovich Sharipin and his wife, Nina, who works in a health polyclinic for children, share the apartment with two of their three grown-up children. Their son Igor Sergeevich works as a doctor at an emergency clinic and his sister Irina Sergeevna is a manager in the logistics department of a company dealing with meat products.

"Many of our neighbours in the buildings around us would like to have their houses renovated the same way as ours has been, with new attic apartments and better environmental economy," Irina says, "but here in Russia all the occupants of a building have to agree 100% to initiate the renovation. Even though our expenses for heating are 65% lower than in the unrenovated buildings, there is always just one person in the blocks who is against any renovation."

Irina, 29, is a manager in the logistics department of a company dealing with meat products, but she still lives in her parents' home.

164

After the renovation, the former slum buildings have become a block of green, attractive apartments. The former narrow backyards have new terraces and plenty of green plants.

A clean environment and recycling: Simmering, Vienna, Austria

Inner city revival, turning old city centres into attractive living spaces, has even spread to areas that have long been considered very unattractive. In Simmering, the eleventh district of Vienna, the capital of Austria, a whole block of worn-down slum-like apartments in an old industrial workers' neighbourhood has been completely reborn as an environment-friendly, energy-saving, green and pleasant place to live.

The district has always been known for its industries. In the 1800s, Simmering generated and supplied the electricity for the trams of Vienna, and had a huge gasworks that supplied the city with gas for its lights. The three old 70-metre tall gasometers once featured in a James Bond movie, but otherwise, as in so many obsolete industrial production centres, the premises were deserted for a quarter of a century until a reconstruction in 2001 converted the structures completely. The three enormous gasometers now contain apartments, offices, a shopping centre and a cinema, and they have become a landmark feature of the district.

Simmering is a far from romantic place. It has a special material-recycling centre, a sewage facility that treats about 90% of the city's sewage, a huge power plant that still supplies Vienna

The large, light-filled apartments in the attic offer the extra charm of green roof terraces with views over Vienna.

The dusty attic of the former slum building has been turned into luxury apartments.

The reborn block of slum apartments in Vienna.

170

with electricity, and a juvenile detention centre.

The reconstruction plan for three worn-down tenement houses focused on changing them into energy-saving, green and pleasant homes for an environment-conscious new generation.

The project was successful; when it was completed, CO_2 emissions had been reduced by 200 tonnes a year and the cost of heating had been reduced by more than 60%.

Many different measures were used to obtain these results: good insulation, new windows with heat-saving features and new doors. Instead of individual heating, the new facilities used heat from the central city system and automatically lowered room temperatures at night. The installation of roof windows in the unused former lofts added to the 'passive solar heating' regulated automatically with blinds.

Another aspect was the use of eco-friendly building materials for all the inner walls and floors, the creation of a green oasis in the form of a central green courtyard like a flying carpet, and many new balconies and terraces full of green plants.

The houses contain a mixture of three- and four-room apartments on the lower floors and large luxury apartments in the once unused and unattractive loft, while the ground floor houses offices and shops that open up to the street to ensure a good mixed, safe environment. Many of the people working there now live in the apartments above.

One thing they enjoy very much in these renovated houses is an aspect of contemporary city living that is often forgotten: space for parking cars, bicycles and children's prams. In this building all these things have been considered, creating an attractive, family-friendly environment.

The old attics have now been transformed into luxury apartments.

Before the renovation: small, dark, worn-down tenements and dirty, narrow backyards.

Staying at home: Franzelarilor, Bucharest, Romania

In a quiet part of the historic area of Bucharest, near the very busy thoroughfare and shopping street Calea Mosilor, is the small street Franzelarilor, named after the first pâtisserie in the city, owned by a Frenchman. The charming houses were built in the period between the two world wars with two floors, large, generous windows and sloping roofs.

This particular building from 1928 was a single-family house. The old loft, like so many other old lofts, was not insulated and was only used for storage. The only light came through a small skylight.

Mihaela Prejmerean, the young daughter of the family living here, decided to renovate the loft and create her own apartment up there, so she started to look around for some inspiration. She called at VELUX Romania for technical advice, as she thought the distance between rafters was too small for a generous window. The attic had a lot of potential, and the architects drew up a design proposal, since it was a great opportunity to create a good example of a renovation project right in the heart of Bucharest.

Although Mihaela initially had a different vision of what the attic should look like, she was convinced after seeing the 3D visu-

Bucharest still has traces of its former beauty and fame as a centre of art. Here, an old glass-covered passage like those in Paris or Milan.

In the busy Calea Mosilor Street, several really old buildings are deteriorating and falling down in complete neglect. A group of young people has started a campaign to save the historical past, photographing and documenting the decaying beauties and showing them all on the Internet in the hope that it will be possible to save them before it is too late.

"I spend some weekends outside, and some others indoors. Unlike other people, I don't have to leave my house in order to refill with energy, because my apartment is lit by so many windows and this makes me feel good and think positively."

alisations, which made her really start to 'see' the space.

The light came in at different times from different angles, so various combinations of roof windows were created to bring the place to life. The whole space revolves around an old chimney, now painted red, so the light coming through the windows takes on a hint of the colour and reflects it. "Even though I did see all the plans, I didn't expect it to look that good – it's as if the space is deciding its own shape. It came out great!" says Mihaela Prejmerean.

Mihaela is not the only person who wants to renovate and rejuvenate the old historic centre of Bucharest. In the busy Calea Mosilor Street, several really old buildings are deteriorating and falling down from complete neglect. A group of young people has started a campaign to save the historical past, photographing and documenting the decaying beauties and showing them all on the Internet in the hope that it will be possible to save them before it is too late.

"My favourite place at home is my studio because it's full of light, and my cats stay with me during my work!"

An artist's studio: Paris, France

In the daylight from her roof windows, artist Florine Asch creates her delicate watercolours.

The daylight from her roof windows is ideal for drawing.

What could be more romantically true to the myth and legend of life in Paris than an artist actually living under the roofs of Paris? What better illustration of the story of light-filled city lofts than the way she uses the daylight coming through the roof windows as she draws her delicate designs and watercolours?

The artist Florine Asch is no fairytale figure, although her works have a certain dreamy, fairytale quality, and she has actually illustrated books of fairytales. But her attractive style is also in great demand from top luxury-product firms and for travel books, cookery books, invitations, menus, children's books and many other purposes.

Florine Asch cannot remember a time when she did not draw. Drawing became more than just a hobby when she got her first job at an auction house in Paris, where she took to sketching the objects before they went under the hammer. Soon she was invited to exhibit at a leading auction house and since then she has never looked back.

Her first real apartment in Paris was this attic apartment. She fell in love with it at first sight: the daylight streaming through the windows was just perfect for her detailed work.

Studio inheritance: Stamboliiski Bul, Sofia, Bulgaria

The old house conceals a beautiful, elegant new attic apartment under the new roof windows.

Old neighbourhoods of Sofia have been torn down, and new shopping complexes and offices are crowding in to replace them. As has happened earlier in many other European cities, the capital of Bulgaria, Sofia, has gone through a phase of 'old is out'. But a new young generation looks at the city centre with different eyes. To them the old housing in the historic centre is a buried treasure to be discovered.

A young married couple, Bozhidar Hinkov and Daniela Slavova, both architects, very much wanted to live in this part of the capital: "The area is in the central part of Sofia and is very close to our jobs at an architectural office; it's near many theatres, cinemas and museums," Daniela explains. "We also save time, and we just don't use the car, we walk!" Bozhidar adds, smiling. Another reason for looking for a loft to convert was its good renovation potential, since apartments in the centre were very expensive.

Fortunately Daniela and Bozhidar did not have to search for long. Bozhidar's father is an artist and his artist's studio in a attic in the old street Stamboliiski Bul was just perfect for them to transform into their dream home. "This place has a sentimental meaning for us, as it was my father's studio," Bozhidar says. "We

From the dining table in the transformed old loft, Daniela and her husband Bozhidar have a great view across Sofia.

A view of Mount Vitosha, the nature reserve nearby, from the central part of Sofia.

Bozhidar likes this place in the apartment best. Here he can see it all....and enjoy watching sport on TV like most other young European men.

180

love this place and call it 'the Studio'".

Just like the young Spanish architects Gálata and Juan in Madrid, these young Bulgarian architects now live in a renovated artist's apartment. And like their Spanish counterparts, they removed the many walls, opening up the area and giving it a feeling of space and comfort. But they chose a very different placing of the roof windows, producing different daylight effects, so the finished result is completely different in style.

"When changing and restoring the apartment, we raised the roof over the lower parts, and we use it as living space now. The small skylights were replaced by roof windows. Now we have plenty of daylight, fresh air and a wonderful view! Above the bathroom we succeeded in creating an extra half-floor and we've put our bedroom there."

"We're a young family and we don't have any children yet (only a dog). As I mentioned, our bedroom is upstairs, and if a child arrives, we'll separate off a small room in the space below the roof windows, so the baby can have plenty of daylight," Daniela smilingly explains.

"My favourite place in our home is on the couch! It is in the centre of the apartment and from this place I can enjoy the light and the view of the whole apartment. And the TV!"

"I love my kitchen and dining-room with VELUX windows above! They give us daylight and a view during the day and the lights of Sofia at night! Last Christmas we gathered together ten people around the table and enjoyed the view!"

"On Sundays we like to walk outside the town in the forest, on the mountain Vitosha where we can also ski six months of the year. We love to play with our dog, play music and take photos. In the near future we plan to buy windsurfing gear and go to the lake to have a sport."

Working
under
the roof

184

Working under the roof

Throughout history daylight has been a key factor in all production and trade, since other kinds of light were scarce and expensive. Most artisans' shops and workshops were open to the street or to the yard through doors and windows to let in as much daylight as possible. Window glass was expensive, so the opening was just a door or a wooden shutter, to be barred at closing time.

Lofts in the city were used for purposes like the storage of grain and other goods, or as stalls for cows kept there by the many brewers of the towns. Beer production had a lot of grain waste as a by-product that could be used as fodder for cows: they often got quite 'drunk', since the mash might contain alcohol. Cows did not take up costly city space when they were parked up in the dark attic, and brewers could offer supplies of milk as well as beer to the city.

As the industrial revolution exploded in the last part of the 1800s, new demands for goods from an increasingly prosperous population changed many workshops into small factories. New, bigger, purpose-built factories were constructed all over Europe as close to the city centres and their workforce as possible and preferably near rivers and waterways so that goods and raw materials could easily be transported.

The big, new factories of the 1800s and 1900s were constructed with huge iron-framed glass windows and skylights so they could use natural daylight for working purposes. Gas lighting was also used, as well as a new and strange phenomenon – electric light – but for a very long time this was far too expensive to use for everyday purposes.

As industrially produced window glass became an affordable commodity, dark city lofts were changed into attractive workplaces for production and trade. Many small production units took over the attic spaces that were now lit by daylight from roof windows. However, they were unpleasantly cold in winter, baking hot in summer, and damp because of leaky steel window frames. Many workplaces had noisy machinery and steam-driven belts, making the workplace a hazardous place to be. In old photos, workplaces might look nostalgically quaint and romantic, but in real life the workplaces were usually nothing of the sort.

Button factory in the attic where daylight is used at the workbenches. The noisy steam-driven belt made the workplace a hazardous place to be.

The Glud and Marstrand enamelware factory. Worktables are placed as close as possible to the roof windows. The electric light is thriftily distributed.

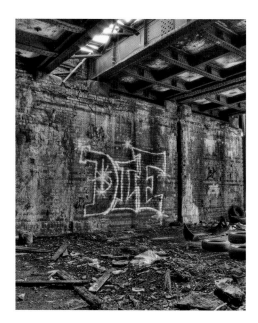

Busy industries in the city centres were deserted in favour of new, purpose-built industrial parks outside the cities. The old factory buildings quickly fell into dilapidation and despair.

The lost city centres

City centres prospered and grew throughout the first part of the twentieth century. But from the 1960s on, new sweeping developments changed city centres within a few years from busy, crowded, prosperous workplaces to desolate run-down wastelands, shunned and deserted. The attics and warehouses of the cities were left as dusty relics of a bygone era, gradually falling into disuse and disrepair.

As industry fled the city centres for modern, spacious production facilities in purpose-built industrial suburbs, this did not mean that daylight became superfluous and disappeared as a production factor. On the contrary, since space was not as confined and restricted as in the inner cities, buildings could spread out. Many new production facilities and factories were laid out in spacious one-storey buildings with skylights rising row upon row like triangular bumper ornaments on the backs of dinosaurs.

But daylight gradually lost out to the new source of light. Electric light became so cheap that many factories preferred it to daylight.

Oil crisis

In 1973 a shock went through the industrialised world: the price of crude oil, then the major energy source, rose steeply. Oil suddenly looked like becoming a scarce resource. Everybody was certain that oil reserves would not be sufficient for more than the next 20 years. From 1993 on, it would be the catastrophic end of the world as we knew it! A lot of solutions were proposed to save oil in order to postpone the disastrous future: car-free Sundays 'saved' on petrol. Houses were to be as well insulated as possible to save on heating. The importance of daylight was forgotten.

So a whole new housing ideal was introduced: thick, insulated walls and minute windows. Daylight disappeared. Electric light replaced daylight. Harsh greyish neon light became standard working light.

Strange as it may sound today, nobody really thought about the consequences of the energy consumed to produce the electricity that was now replacing daylight.

Electric light replaced daylight. Harsh greyish neon light became the standard working light. Strange as it may sound today, nobody really thought about the consequences of the energy consumed to produce the electricity that replaced daylight.

The industrial inner city revival

At the end of the twentieth century, a new generation looked at the run-down, deserted industrial wastelands of city centres from a completely different perspective. The towering, imposing structures of early industrialisation, the city lofts and attics, all seemed to them to represent opportunities for providing creative, light-filled spaces so very different from the standard uniformity of the neon-grey offices.

Lofts and attics have taken on new life as workplaces for the production of a new age: the creative industries have taken over the old attic spaces. Where the deafening noise of machines or crowded workshops once filled the spaces under the city roofs, information providers now work at their computers or hold meetings while daylight from roof windows fills the bright rooms, creating optimal working conditions for a new age.

188

Jugend malls: Hackescher Markt, Berlin, Germany

The beautiful Jugend-style buildings have taken on new, original life as a shopping and restaurant centre.

A visit to Berlin in Germany often includes the Spandauer neighbourhood of Berlin Mitte with the Hackesche Höfe complex, a labyrinth of courtyards brimming with cafés, restaurants, boutiques and art galleries. The local railway station on the city line looks more like a grand palace or museum. Constructed at the height of the railway boom in the late 1800s with a huge dome, a red-tiled façade, mosaics and rounded windows, it is an expression of the former wealth and importance of the place.

The Hackesche Höfe area is a typical example of how a European city has changed over time. Originally, in medieval times, the area was a swamp between two bastions in the defensive walls of Berlin, a place of busy market trading outside the city gates. As the industrial revolution took hold, new businesses and booming industries set up shops there.

Then, during the boom years at the beginning of the 1900s, Germany's biggest shopping/entertainment/housing/industrial area was constructed there. The new invention, the motion picture cinema, was a crowd-drawer; new industries and busy factories boasted the most modern and ornate appearances, and luxurious department stores offered an unheard-of variety of goods.

The imposing railway station was constructed at the height of the railway boom in the late 1800s. With a huge dome, a red-tiled façade, mosaics and rounded windows, it is an expression of the former wealth and importance of the place.

The modern offices in the attic of the restored building are located in a lively, inviting part of Berlin with many restaurants and cafés.

The best and most fashionable architects designed imposing features in the Jugend style of the times. All through the roaring twenties and thirties, the complex was at the heart of the famous, lively Berlin scene. Then the war changed everything.

At the end of the Second World War, Berlin was a city in ruins. A few years later, when Germany was divided in two states, East and West Germany, Berlin was truncated, split into two halves, East and West Berlin. The division culminated in the construction of the Berlin Wall, which made any communication between the two halves impossible. Hackesche Höfe became part of East Berlin and was renamed Marx-Engels-Platz in the Socialist era of the new German Democratic Republic (GDR).

When Socialist GDR fell in 1989, the Berlin Wall was torn down. Germany was once again united, and all of Berlin became one city, again the capital of the country. A remarkable building frenzy changed the cityscape. New buildings and complexes were seen everywhere. Old dilapidated areas were lovingly restored and renewed, including the Hackesche Höfe with its beautiful

Jugend-style features, once again appreciated by the crowds frequenting the area. This change coincided with the new European focus on the qualities of old industrial inner city districts.

On the corner of Hackesche, a commercial complex was originally a busy part of the whole area. During the Cold War era, the complex was turned into private apartments and allowed to fall into disrepair and become a slum.

After the demolition of the Berlin Wall, the complex was declared a protected historic monument, a Baudenkmal. Between 2001 and 2003 a thorough clearance and rebuilding process took place. Missing parts of the building were reconstructed; the façade, two staircases and the inside structures were restored to their original splendour. Under the auspices of the preservation authority, the Denkmalschutz, the roof from the 1960s was taken down and rebuilt in a steeper, more original angle. The Denkmalschutz recommended large studio windows in the roof, and a solution was found using 120 zinc-framed roof windows, all electrically operated and with built-in sunscreens.

Hackesche Höfe has once again become a vibrant, prosperous part of the city. Art, culture, apartments, trade and industry, gastronomy and entertainment fill the city neighbourhood. But in the hidden corners and corridors of the busy warrens of the Hackescher complex, you can still find graffiti – now more as a nostalgic reminiscence of the 'good old slum days of East Berlin'.

The roofs of Berlin and the Television Tower landmark can be seen through the roof windows from the conference room.

The huge roof windows in the restored house make
for a pleasant workplace filled with daylight,
regulated by automatic sunscreens.

IT and democracy: Assembleia da República, Lisbon, Portugal

Lisbon, the atmospheric and colourful capital of Portugal, is situated like an amphitheatre on hillsides by the mouth of river Tagus flowing into the Atlantic. It has a more than 3,000-year-old history, founded as it was by Phoenician traders who saw the possibilities of its natural harbour in its protected position. Vasco da Gama set sail from Lisbon in 1497 when he went on his first voyage and discovered the sea-route from Europe to India around the Cape of Good Hope, and the history of the city as the richest centre of the silver trade with the New World colonies in South America has left its mark on the city. The long, rich past and the pleasant climate make Lisbon a beautiful experience and a good place to live.

The Portuguese Parliament convenes in the Palácio de São Bento in the centre of Lisbon. Originally a Benedictine monastery, the palace has been rebuilt and changed several times in the course of its history. A parliament building is a huge workplace, and as in all other workplaces, the need for information technology exploded a few years ago. But how does one find space in an old palace for an IT department? All the space and rooms in the Palácio de São Bento were in use – except the loft, which was used for storage. So in 2003 the whole attic floor underwent a complete change. The many roof windows create a bright, pleasant environment, and automatic sunscreens in the windows take care of the indoor climate, filtering sunshine before it becomes too hot. Some of the roof windows also open automatically to allow ventilation when necessary.

The Portuguese Parliament is a huge workplace, and as in all other workplaces, the need for information technology exploded a few years ago. The only space available was the old, unused attic and here the staff of the IT-department work in pleasant, bright offices, where natural ventilation and the sharp daylight are automatically regulated by sunscreened roof windows.

Music in the docks: Islands Brygge, Copenhagen, Denmark

Copenhagen, like many cities in Europe, is currently rediscovering its waterfront. Islands Brygge ('the Iceland Wharf'), a former industrial and docks district in the eastern part of the city centre, is at the core of this magic transformation. The dirty industrial factories and workplaces have been superseded by milieux for the young, creative and affluent, while feverish construction activity has replaced the desolate industrial facilities and ruins. Warehouses have been converted. Industries of a new age compete for a place here. An old zeppelin hangar from Berlin has been turned into the headquarters of an IT company. Two circular, former silos right next to the water have been converted into apartment towers for the wealthy. And new glass-façaded, balconied apartment buildings sprout up along the waterfront park.

City harbours used to be associated with slums, sewage sludge, algae growth and oil spill. And that is just what it used to be like here too. Now there is a city park along the waterfront of Islands Brygge, offering an open seawater swimming pool in the clean, clear water of the harbour. It is pretty rare to find natural saltwater public swimming areas in the middle of a major city. No wonder Islands Brygge has been called one of the world's best waterfronts. People lounge on the grass in huge numbers – friends, families, kids enjoying life; a number of new cafés have opened up; and on a hot spring or summer day (or even just an average one), the area teems with life.

This is a far cry from the Islands Brygge of the 1970s, which had fallen into the same sort of desolation and dilapidation as other European waterfront industrial districts. The place was shunned by everyone except fashion photographers hunting for backdrops of authentically putrid city despair.

One of the former dilapidated industrial buildings is now home to the Mogens Dahl Concert Hall that offers master classes in song, piano and conducting as well as jazz, choir and chamber music concerts. The large concert hall is filled with soft, accentu-

The former industrial wharf area of Islands Brygge is a most attractive part of Copenhagen today. On summer days, crowds of Copenhageners chill out in the park along the quays and enjoy swimming in the new pool in the now clean water of the former harbour. Or they just jump in freestyle from the wharfs.

The former car-repair workshop had its attic opened up completely and today houses the Mogens Dahl Concert Hall.

ated daylight. Four new roof window turrets have been installed. The direct light from the south is diffused by large alabaster-glass windows, while the indirect light from the north, reflected from the neighbouring fire wall, enters through smaller windows with clear glass.

This seems very far from the origin of the building. A hundred years ago the main building was built for a printing company, the present concert hall was a stable to horses and coaches and later in the century the building was used for decades as a car repair and paintshop. The first floor was divided by a succession of partition walls into small rooms, jam-packed with spare parts. Before the conversion, the only daylight came through a few vertical windows.

"Usually, the audience in concert halls is a long way from the musicians," Mogens Dahl says. "But here people can see all the details, smell the wooden instruments, hear the breathing of the musicians and the turning of the pages of the score. And the musicians sense every change in the mood of their audience. This kind of direct feedback is so important."

The Mogens Dahl Concert Hall is a workplace of a new age: it is used for numerous activities like conferences, shows, meetings and workshops – and of course concerts.

Railway romance: Gymnase du Bugnon, Flon, Lausanne, Switzerland

Lausanne, Switzerland – perhaps you start imagining quaint old city streets with flower-filled fountains and picture-postcard views of Lac Leman – Lake Geneva. But right in the city centre, you can see a completely different perspective, more reminiscent of the scenery from a futuristic film: busy roads crossing utilitarian bridges around a large 'hole' in the ground. The hole in the ground is the Flon district, a large, rough-looking entertainment area filled with restaurants, chic bars and trendy art galleries, discos, cafés and a college, all housed in former warehouses and industries.

The trendy look of the Flon is very, very new. A former railway warehouse centre for the busy railway line from Lausanne centre to the port on Lake Geneva, it lost its importance, like so many other European industrial centres, from the 1960s on. A completely deserted and dilapidated slum, in 2003-2006 the whole district underwent a transformation into the hottest spot in southern Switzerland. But since many of these changes are still unfinished, the street culture in the area still co-exists with the trendy crowd. Some of the former street culture has become established events – like the International Skateboarding Grand Prix.

A former warehouse has been transformed into a high school for young people. In order to function as an educational building, the large openings in the façades were enlarged further and the roof windows were placed close together, permitting the use of a second floor.

The reborn entertainment area of Flon is home to many creative industries and art initiatives.

In the Flon district, a former warehouse for building materials from the 1930s has been transformed into a new home for the high school Gymnase du Bugnon. Where stacks of bricks, mortar, windows and doors used to fill the bare spaces, young students in their last school years now crowd through rooms in contemporary design. Eagerly engaged in the project 'Generation 07', they participate in debates, blogs and webcasts on society of the future and the politics that will take them there.

Changing the sparse, industrial halls into a living environment required a lot of imagination and practical sense. The architects involved aimed at preserving as much as possible of the original, strictly functional character, while also giving it a feeling of contemporary design and comfort.

The contemporary feeling is produced by the yellowish-green neon colours pervading the public areas. But the most contemporary aspect of the design is not really visible: the whole reconstruction process has been done according to the strict environmental ideals of the 'Minergie code', which involves creating an extra high-quality energy environment with air conditioning and noise reduction.

This aspect of their new school is the one most appreciated by the students – Generation 07 is highly aware of the environmental challenges of the future.

War and peace: Stup, Sarajevo, Bosnia-Herzegovina

The war-ravaged house near Sarajevo has been completely restored and reborn into a peaceful light-filled working place.

The photo exudes peace, light and tranquillity: a young, pregnant woman is reaching up to put the finishing touch to a lamp in an attic filled with soft daylight; a subject so very far removed from the other picture of a burnt-down, war-ravaged house with bare rafters sticking out. And yet the pictures are of the same house in the same place, but taken twelve years apart. These are two pictures of the fate of the country of Bosnia-Herzegovina, ravaged by a cruel civil war in 1992-95.

The house is in Stup, a former village that grew into an industrial suburb along the main road to the Bosnian city of Sarajevo. As civil war exploded, Sarajevo witnessed the longest siege in the history of modern warfare; during the almost four years of the cruel siege, Stup was right on the road that became known as 'Sniper Alley'. In Sarajevo the continuous bombs and snipers' bullets took a huge toll – almost 12,000 dead and 50,000 wounded. And yet the citizens endured the hardships of the siege despite the scarcity of food, heat and safety.

Today, Sarajevo is once again a prosperous, peaceful city. And this small, ordinary house now contains offices; the attic has been restored twice and opened up to daylight by the many roof windows. The new generations of Bosnia-Herzegovina are looking forward to a peaceful future.

Inside the same house – 12 years later.

A chocolate jungle in the hayloft: Ørsholt, Denmark

The rolling, green hills with farmland, fruit trees, copses and horse paddocks in northern Zealand, Denmark, seem very far from the hot, humid jungle of the Caribbean island of Hispaniola. And yet, hidden in a former hayloft at the Ørsholt manor house, cocoa trees are in bloom, and mature pods hang from the trunks.

The former manor house has been completely changed and rebuilt by the owner Peter Beier to house his ruling passion: the production of the undiluted, pure pleasure of authentic chocolate. "I want to know my products, and the only way to do that properly is to produce them all the way from the raw materials to the end products," Peter Beier explains. The first step was to buy a cocoa plantation, so he checked out the best chocolate-producing countries in Central America, using four criteria: first, as a Dane he had to be able to buy a plantation legally; second, the chocolate produced had to be of prime quality; third, the place had to be safe; and fourth, he had to like the country and feel welcome. In the Dominican Republic, on the island of Hispaniola, Peter Beier found just what he was looking for.

"Passion is the driving force for me," he says. "I want the people working with me to share this passion. Chocolate shouldn't just be 'something they produce'. The only way to feel that passion is to know what you are dealing with." And that is why he took a bit of the jungle from Hispaniola and transferred it to cold Denmark so his staff could learn about and experience what chocolate really is.

Not an easy task, as cocoa plants need lots and lots of very strong sunlight, a temperature of 30 degrees Celsius and a constant humidity of 80-90%. All these conditions were created in the loft of the huge roof construction of the former barn.

Entering the room, you feel bathed in strong light from the twenty large roof windows in the huge, sloping, south-facing ceiling. All the windows are of course automatically operated.

208

210

During the dark winter half of the year, the weak Danish daylight is not sufficient, so strong solar spotlights supply the necessary light.

And then, there they are, the 'chocolate trees'. The trunk of one tree is covered with row upon row of small, fragrant flowers; from another tree trunk, oblong yellow and green melon-like cocoa fruits hang. To a European, it is strange to see fruit growing from the trunk, while the branches only bear large, light leaves. Banana palms grow in pots among the cocoa trees of all sizes, as on Hispaniola. Cocoa pods from the plantation were brought back to Denmark; the seeds were extracted and planted in pots, and now new small cocoa plants are sprouting all over the floor. This is Criolla cocoa, the variety called Evido. Each tree in Peter Beier's plantation in the Dominican Republic produces 1 kg of chocolate a year. Just now he is experimenting with a new variety which he hopes will produce two kilos a year. The first results will not be seen until 4-5 years' time.

"I hope to give something back to the country that has let me have the privilege of pursuing my passion," Peter Beier says. "The best way to do that is by introducing methods that bring better harvest yields to the people there, which they can use in their own production. I also found that the conventional method of drying the cocoa beans meant that more than 20% was lost to chickens and rats, because the beans were dried on the bare earth. So we built covered drying shelves which effectively keep the pests away. Now most of my neighbours use them too."

Peter Beier's passion for pure raw materials never stops. At Ørsholt he is experimenting with fruit-growing for the production of the soft, natural fruit fillings in his chocolates. So far he has planted fifteen different apple sorts, eight prune and plum sorts, twelve cherry sorts, five pear sorts, four vine sorts, crab apples, brambles, strawberries and raspberries. All of course organically grown.

Meanwhile the small green cocoa trees in the former hayloft continue to grow at the tropical speed of 1-2 metres a year under the roof windows in this country far to the north.

The former manor house has been completely changed and rebuilt by owner Peter Beier to house his ruling passion: the production of the undiluted, pure pleasure of authentic chocolate.

He brought a bit of the jungle from his cocoa plantation on the tropical island of Hispaniola to cold Denmark so his staff could learn about and experience what chocolate really is. "I want to know my products, and the only way to do that properly is to produce them all the way from the raw materials to the end products."

The old red-brick house had been used by the Navy for storage purposes ever since it was built in 1872: first for gunpowder, then for sea mines, then for grain and then just for plain old junk. Later, when the house became a private storage building, it fell into disrepair.

From gunpowder to web shop: Kristiansand, Sørlandet, Norway

Sørlandet (the southland) in Norway holds the Norwegian record for hours of sunlight. The mild coastal climate and thousands of tiny islands and fjords make it perfect for boating and fishing, so the area is a favourite holiday destination for many Norwegians. Kristiansand is a small picture-postcard town, for centuries a military stronghold dominating the passage between Norway and northern Denmark. In recent history it even played an important role in the Second World War.

This particular red-brick house had been used by the Navy for storage purposes ever since it was built in 1872. First for gunpowder, then for sea mines, then for grain, and then just for plain old junk. Later, when the house became a private storage building, it fell into disrepair.

Today the old gunpowder magazine has been turned into an attractive workplace for an Internet-based web firm selling design objects for kitchens and bathrooms. The interior has been transformed by enhancing the strong, rough-brick Navy construction with heavy oak beams combined with an original pattern of roof windows. The old warehouse was dark and gloomy with tiny windows, and not very suitable for offices in a modern workplace. Today the premises are suffused with daylight from the ingeniously placed roof windows. In one part of the roof, the windows along the ridge beam give the impression that the house is open to the sky, while in another part large Cabrio windows create balconies enabling the people working for the company to enjoy the sunny climate.

Holding creative meetings under the sky is a feature of the web-based company.

Giant roofs: Faculty of Architecture, University of Technology, Gdańsk, Poland

The huge loft was only used by pigeons before the renovation. The dust from their excrement spread through the air in the ventilation shafts and posed a serious health risk for students and teachers.

Gdańsk is a prosperous old port on Poland's Baltic coast. In 2004 the Gdańsk University of Technology celebrated its centenary and used the occasion as an opportunity to carry out a thorough modernisation. The aim was to provide students and professors with better conditions – and they were sorely needed. The old building with the enormous roof was originally built in 1904 in historicising Flemish Renaissance and Baroque style, and was listed in the register of historic monuments.

In one part of the building, the supporting steel frame had been seriously deformed as a result of the fire in 1945 after the liberation of Gdańsk. Some parts of the steel frames, even those that had been twisted in the high temperatures during the fire, were used in the reconstruction of the university after the war. Since the structure was not properly protected from corrosion, it deteriorated and was in serious danger of collapsing.

The building also posed significant health risks: students and teachers were breathing in air from the ventilation ducts leading down from the huge loft, where only pigeons lived. The ventilation system too had been damaged during the war and had not been maintained, so the classrooms and offices were being filled

The old centre of Gdańsk has been lovingly restored.

The renovation of the loft of the Gdańsk University of Technology provided a staggering extra area of 2,500 m^2.

Students in the Department of Drawing and Painting profit greatly from the new, daylight-filled studios under the giant roof.

220

The student areas are filled with bright daylight from the large roof windows, a favourite place for working and discussing.

with air polluted by a hundred years of pigeon droppings!

Before reconstruction, the roof was clad only in old roof tiles, and the ceiling under the attic was made of uninsulated reinforced concrete. Thermal losses were so great that the heating system was completely inefficient. A new glass roof now covers the whole internal courtyard, and together with the insulation of the attic this makes for a pleasant indoor climate and a much lower heating budget.

The renovation of the loft gave the university a staggering 2,500 m² of extra space to use; unfortunately, it still lacks the funding for equipment to be able to use it all. Only the Department of Health and the Department of Drawing and Painting are profiting greatly from studying and working in daylight under the giant roof.

Preserving
historic
heritage

Preserving historic heritage

The historic heritage of Europe is simply overwhelming. Wherever you turn, you see traces of the past. Buildings and structures centuries and even millennia old can be found in incredible numbers: imposing castles, military fortresses, churches, manor houses, palaces, quaint cafés, whole city neighbourhoods of streets and houses, industrial workers' homes, country cottages, farmhouses and deserted fishermen's huts.

What should be done about this enormous European heritage? Of course some of it is taken care of by local or national authorities, and has now been given a purpose as museums or monuments so it can be preserved for future generations. Some historic buildings have remained in use ever since their construction centuries ago. But how do we ensure that heritage is preserved while adapting old buildings to become a living part of contemporary life? Other buildings and structures have just been left in the landscape as dying debris until individuals or groups take an interest in their preservation and contemporary use and change them into beautiful swans.

A huge challenge faces anyone taking up the challenge of preserving heritage while allowing for its function in a contemporary context as a living part of society. In all European countries, local and central bodies have been created to protect the historic heritage. They may function as monitors and buffers against vandalism, but more often they are advisory boards, giving inspiration and ideas to architects challenged with changing part or the whole of historic structures, as well as to private individuals interested in changing their property in harmony with its past.

This chapter on preserving historic heritage is about changes undertaken in the larger and more spectacular structures, like fortresses in Russia and France, and castles in France and Belgium; as well as changes made to save modest Victorian terraced workers' houses, a hippie-occupied historic defence complex in Copenhagen, an aristocratic villa in the Czech Republic, a shooting gallery in Hungary and a sea captain's house in Brittany.

These are all stories about how changes involving roof windows are enabling historic buildings and structures to function in a modern context – while preserving heritage.

Some other chapters in this book, notably 'Changing the home' and 'Lighting up the city loft', offer more examples of private homeowners' cooperation with local heritage boards.

Centuries of health care: Hôtel Dieu, Paris, France

For the incredible timespan of almost 1,400 years, since the year 651, the ancient hospital Hôtel Dieu has existed on the Île de la Cité in the heart of Paris. At a time when the rest of Europe was living through the barbarian ages, here in Paris a charity led by a monastery took care of the sick and the old in this first hospital in France. For almost 800 years it remained the only one.

The present buildings of the Hôtel Dieu (it means 'The Guest House of God') are not so ancient: they date from the later part of the 1800s. The hospital is still one of the elite hospitals of France and is still on exactly the same site as in ancient times!

Space is scarce in the old hospital, so windows have been installed in all the roofs to permit use of the loft space. Since Hôtel Dieu is right next to the famous Notre Dame Cathedral, the ability of the windows to blend in without disturbing the famous heritage architecture is of the utmost importance.

Notre Dame Cathedral in Paris with the roofs of Hôtel Dieu in the foreground.

The ancient hospital Hôtel Dieu has been on this same site in Paris for more than 1,400 years. The present buildings of the hospital are almost 'new', only about 150 years old. All roofs of the Hôtel Dieu hospital complex have roof windows so that better use can be made of the available space.

The Palais de Justice occupies more than four hectares of land and has almost 200,000 m² of space.

During the French Revolution, Queen Marie-Antoinette was imprisoned in the Conciergerie section of the Palais de Justice before her execution. And in the deep dungeons of the medieval Palais de Justice, dark torture chambers still exude an atmosphere of cruelty and suffering.

Centuries of power: Palais de Justice, Paris, France

Ever since the age of the Roman Empire two thousand years ago, the centre of power in Paris has been in the oldest part of the town on the Île de la Cité, one of the islands in the middle of the Seine. You sense a special continuity down through millennia when you walk through the area today, as do most visitors and tourists when they visit Notre Dame, the magnificent Sainte Chapelle or the gardens of the Palais Royal. The buildings have been changed and rebuilt again and again through the ages to match the taste of the day, but they have functioned continuously as centres of power in Paris.

During the French Revolution, doomed aristocrats waited in queues in the cellars and courtyards of the Conciergerie in the Palais de Justice to be driven to the guillotine in a never-ending procession of horsedrawn carts , while the mob jeered at them in a bloodthirsty frenzy. Queen Marie-Antoinette was imprisoned there before being moved to an even more secure place before her execution. And in the deep dungeons of the medieval Palais de Justice, dark torture chambers still exude an atmosphere of cruelty and suffering.

In one of the courts of the Palais de Justice is the Sainte Chapelle, a miraculously light-filled Gothic masterpiece with high walls of glowing, multi-coloured stained-glass windows. The almost impossible floating lightness of the building was created in 1248 by order of King Louis IX, also known as 'Saint Louis'; this was where he prayed for the success of his crusades to Jerusalem.

The Palais de Justice is a huge complex, a workplace for four thousand magistrates and civil servants, and all the attics are used for administrative purposes today. The first VELUX roof windows in the Palais de Justice were installed many years ago, and ever since, new types of windows have been developed in cooperation with architects specialising in historic buildings: in different sizes and colours, and in forms that can be integrated into the roof without protruding elements.

In the gardens of the Palais Royal, businesspeople in formal suits, students, lawyers and civil servants from the surrounding offices relax, play a game of boules or just enjoy an hour of peace at lunchtime.

Centuries of fun:
Jardin du Palais Royal, Paris, France

Opposite the enormous museum complex of the Louvre is a large haven of peace and relaxation: the Baroque-styled gardens of the Palais Royal, where businesspeople in formal suits, students, lawyers and civil servants from the surrounding offices relax, play a game of boules or just enjoy an hour of peace at lunchtime.

This atmosphere of pleasant relaxation and pleasure has a long tradition behind it. The Palace was built in 1624 as a private home of the Prime Minister of France, Cardinal Richelieu (the 'villain' of The Three Musketeers). Inside the Palace was the most modern theatre of the day, with the first moving scenery to be seen in France, and it was there, later in the century, that the famous French playwright Molière and his troupe performed his comedies for the court of the Duke of Orleans, the brother of King Louis XIV. The Palace acquired quite a reputation of scandal and debauchery as the Duke preferred young men to his wife, who responded by indulging in a series of liaisons. The whole court revelled in parties, carnivals and lavish banquets, and provided material for much of the gossip and talk of the day.

The Palace continued to house a variety of royal and aristocratic theatres and places of entertainment, and in the nineteenth century the then new buildings surrounding the garden housed luxury boutiques in the arcades. Today the arcades are full of restaurants, galleries and delicatessens. The present huge palace complex of buildings is home to the French Ministry of Culture and the Council of State, so today the fun has been relegated to the gardens!

Everywhere in Paris space is scarce, so all the loft floors of the palace have been transformed into office spaces. In the roof, three generations of VELUX windows testify to how the roof windows have increasingly been adapted to this precious heritage.

In the formal courtyard, a modern work of art, striped columns by the artist Daniel Buren, enraged the Parisians when it was finished in the 1990s, but since then the black and white columns have been used by young people enjoying a break from work.

Gambling, shooting, swimming and drinking: Café Zila, Pestszentlörinc, Hungary

After winning an incredible fortune gambling in a casino in Vienna in 1902 in the age of the Austro-Hungarian Empire, the Hungarian Count Miklós Szemere returned to Hungary. He bought the huge Cséry estates for most of his winnings, and spent the rest living a very comfortable life.

His greatest passion after gambling was shooting, so on the estate he had a shooting gallery built. The gallery was meant for practicing shooting as a sport, and to his great joy a whole generation of sports shooters who trained there won prizes in national and international competitions.

However, local people did not enjoy the shooting as much as the counts of Cséry and their guests, probably because the bullets of the shooting parties hit other things than their targets. Following several accidents, the local authorities declared the shooting range dangerous and closed it down. Years later, when the huge estate was divided up after the demise of the Count, the village insisted on keeping the former shooting gallery, intending to convert the surrounding area into an outdoor pool complex. The building was then redesigned and served as changing rooms for swimmers for fifty years until as recently as 1998.

In 1998 the pastry chef László Zila bought the swimming complex, and a year later added the changing rooms, Count Szemere's former shooting gallery. He wanted to restore the original appearance of the building and preserve the typical German Fachwerk style – redwood with brick infill – for the guests and for the future.

The high ceiling of the shooting gallery just cried out for the creation of a mezzanine; a long row of roof windows was installed in the woodwork, and you can now admire the restored beauty of the place while enjoying the tasty, delicate pastries and ice cream of the pastry chef.

The shooting gallery was meant for practicing shooting as a sport; a whole generation of sports shooters trained there and won prizes in national and international competitions. Local people did not enjoy the shooting as much as the counts of Cséry and their guests, since the bullets of the shooting parties hit other things than their targets.

The former shooting gallery has been lovingly restored to show the German brick and wood 'Fachwerk' style. A new mezzanine floor and roof windows create ample space for customers to enjoy the delicate cakes of Café Zila.

A Baltic jewel set in gold: the Peter-Paul Fortress, St. Petersburg, Russia

In fairytales, cities have turrets of shining gold – in real life, cities do not, except for the real city of St. Petersburg on the shore of the Baltic Sea, where soaring golden spires, golden domes, golden turrets topped by golden angels and golden crosses are everywhere to be seen. Under the often cold, grey northern sky, the golden architecture pointing to the heavens captures the daylight and the reflections from the surrounding sea and canals as an inner glow. The gold is set off by the impossibly beautiful buildings in intense colours: the yellow of the Peter-Paul Fortress and the Admiralty; the turquoise-green of the Winter Palace Hermitage Museum; the red, the pink, the eggshell blue and more yellow again from the mansions, churches and palaces everywhere. Even roofs are coloured: green on yellow houses, yellow on blue, grey on red, blue on pink houses. The colours are given a floating lightness by the white frames around doors and windows and the geometrical ornaments adorning large parts of the façades.

The whole city centre was planned and for the most part built in the 1700s in Baroque and Rococo style before later fashions turned the preferred colours of northern cities into the rather

In fairytales, cities have turrets of shining gold – in real life, cities do not, except for the real city of St. Petersburg on the shores of the Baltic Sea, where soaring golden spires, golden domes, golden turrets topped by golden angels and golden crosses are everywhere to be seen.

242

subdued grey, brown or white colours of today.

Most of the St. Petersburg city centre has been restored to its former glory after eighty years of total neglect during the Communist era, when the city was called Leningrad. When Putin became President of Russia, the city awoke from its sleep, because Putin saw to it that his home town regained the glory of its period as the capital of imperial Russia.

In 1703, when the Russian Tsar Peter the Great planned a city bearing his name in the cold, humid swamps at the mouth of the river Neva on the Baltic coast, he called in the best of European architects, artists and military designers. The first building erected was the Peter-Paul Fortress, because this was to be the stronghold ensuring the Russian fleet access to the Baltic Sea. The European countries around the Baltic had fought bitterly cruel wars for domination for most of the preceding hundred years, and the superpower of the day, Sweden, ruled over most of the northern shores.

Artisans and labourers from all over Russia were forced to move to the new city, and Peter the Great invited craftsmen and traders from the whole of Europe to settle in his new imperial city. Land was given away free; every European settler was even given a free workshop and ten Russian apprentices. Thus a whole generation of Russian designers and builders learned the latest techniques and styles, using them to build the rapidly expanding city. Russian nobles were obliged to build a house or palace befitting their positions, and when St. Petersburg became the capital of Russia in 1713 the whole court moved to the city and competed to build the most beautiful palaces. For 200 years, St. Petersburg remained the imperial capital of Russia, until the Russian Revolution in 1918, when Moscow was chosen as capital of the new Communist regime.

The Peter-Paul Fortress was such a strong defensive citadel that it was never attacked. Today it is one of the 'must-sees' of the many tourists from the whole world who flock to this jewel of the Baltic during 'the white nights' in June when it never gets dark, only taking on a glowing rosy hue for a few hours around midnight. By contrast, during the dark half of the year the sun is hardly seen in St. Petersburg – one of the reasons for an intense desire to let as much daylight as possible into the houses.

Tourism requires information and administration, and in the

The Peter-Paul Fortress is one of the top visitors' attractions in St. Petersburg. Here, a class of young Russian students from a military academy.

Today the area outside the walls is open to the public, and the residents of St. Petersburg like to use it to enjoy the sunshine whenever possible in this northern city.

Today the 'St. John Ravelin' of the Peter-Paul fortress peacefully houses the information and documentation centre of the Peter-Paul Fortress. A ravelin was a special kind of fortress architecture in the bastions providing better defences against an attacking enemy.

The visitors' centre and the information and documentation centre of the fortress are located in the former soldiers' quarters in one of the ravelins. Here the Head of the Information Zone, Irina Karuseva, enjoys working in the daylight from the windows in the almost flat roof of the former ravelin.

former military quarters in one of the fortified units of the fortress known as the 'ravelins', offices have been created. The St. John Ravelin was constructed in place of the original earth-and-wood structure. Today Irina Karuseva, head of the Information Zone in the Museum of the History of St. Petersburg, works here in the daylight streaming through VELUX windows in the almost flat roof of the ravelin. Seen from outside, the windows blend in almost unnoticeably with the beauty of the red, yellow and golden complexes of the inner courtyards, where the golden spire of the Peter-Paul Church stands guard over the remains of the Tsars of Russia.

244

Hippie nostalgia: the Free City of Christiania, Copenhagen, Denmark

When you walk around the idyllic surroundings of Christiania, just outside the centre of Copenhagen, you find yourself in some of the best preserved European city defence works of the 1600s, with bastions, moats and ramparts. It is hard to imagine that this place has often made headlines in the media as a result of conflict and rioting.

The area was part of the defences of Copenhagen for centuries, but in 1971, when the military moved out, it was left to decline and dilapidation. A group of hippie squatters moved in and declared Christiania a 'free city'. The place mainly became known for its free hash market and as a place where you could pick up 'hot' items.

The colourful, rebellious past of the free city is just a memory today. The former hash market, 'Pusher Street', has been closed down: cafés, an up-market bicycle shop and souvenir knick-knacks have replaced the drug pushers. The most dangerous things on sale today may be gourd chillums, incense, tie-dyed scarves or Indian dream-catcher pendulums. The majority of the residents of Christiania today are well-established artists, craftsmen and civil servants, most of them with jobs in the city outside. In some corners near the main entrance, you can still find a slum-like look and misery, if you look closely, and some dropouts, junkies and alcoholics still live in huge, desolate former military barracks.

"The last stand against the privileges of heritage and nobility", the creed of Christiania is sometimes ironically called. In Christiania, the privilege of living in a huge, green, romantic, idyllic heritage area is granted only to families and friends of the 'council' of original settlers. Woe betide anyone who tries to build a new, small home on the canals, as some youngsters did a few years ago on a candid camera show! Like noble families of

the past, the original residents defend their privileges. Demands from the state for property taxes are regarded as undue interference in private affairs. But like the nobility of the olden times, even Christiania has had to yield: today the inhabitants do pay for electricity, water and sanitation.

Christiania is now one of the most frequently visited tourist attractions in Copenhagen, surpassed only by the amusement park Tivoli! The Christmas Market in particular is a famous, well-loved event.

Most of the buildings in Christiania are lovingly restored old military barracks, gunpowder magazines, bastions or self-designed houses in sizes from huts to mansions. The 'home-grown' architecture of Christiania has become a famous trend, even an inspiration in pictures in fancy coffee-table books.

One of the original values of the free city was to be as environmentally aware as possible. An emphasis on recycling means that Christiania has one of the biggest outlets for used building materials like windows, doors, bricks or timber. And as a consequence, incorporated in the houses of Christiania, you find one of the most extensive selections of succeeding generations of VELUX windows!

The 'home-grown' architecture of Christiania has become a famous trend, even an inspiration shown in pictures in fancy coffee-table books.

The old military buildings on the green bastions have been restored by the Christianites, and most of them have roof windows in the attics. Today Christiania is one of the most frequently visited tourist attractions in Copenhagen, only surpassed by the amusement park Tivoli!

One particularly successful feature of the free city is the 'Christiania bikes'. Produced in the free city, these bicycles have become an 'in' statement of young Copenhageners and their favourite means of transporting their children around the inner city.

252

Knights' tales and storytellers: Landcommanderij Alden Biesen, Limburg, Belgium

The castle was a stronghold of the German crusading Knights of the Teutonic Order.

In the huge castle complex of the Landcommanderij Alden Biesen in Belgium, you inevitably meet groups of young people from all over Europe. This Flemish cultural centre has a strong focus on activities, seminars and conferences for children and young people. Each year in May, the castle looks rather like Hogwarts, the school where Harry Potter (of the famous fantasy books) spent his schooldays. The whole castle resounds with fantastic stories and fairytales as children and teenagers from hundreds of schools all over Europe meet at the Storytelling Festival for nine days. For the Flemish youngsters, the stories are in Dutch, but from the age of 16 on they can choose from Dutch, English, French and German. The 2007 festival with 35 storytellers, 180 hours of storytelling, 12,000 people and 19,000 tickets turned the Alden Biesen festival into one of the largest storytelling festivals in Europe.

It is difficult to imagine a more fitting place for storytelling than the 'Landcommanderij' of Alden Biesen. The castle complex was built by the German Knights of the Teutonic Order more than a thousand years ago. The Knights were an order of crusaders who took care of sick and wounded soldiers, something few

In the park the magical millennium oak was a young tree when the castle was built a thousand yeas ago.

The Flemish cultural centre of Alden Biesen has a strong focus on activities, seminars and conferences for children and young people. Each year in May, during the huge storytelling festival, the castle almost resembles Hogwarts, the school where Harry Potter (of the famous fantasy books) spent his schooldays.

people cared about at that time. As time passed, the order became very rich and powerful and built many strongholds all over Europe.

The castle has been changed and rebuilt throughout the centuries, but perhaps most thoroughly after 1971, when the state acquired it after a serious fire and had it restored to create the present cultural centre. One practical aspect of changing a former knights' stronghold into a meeting and conference facility is where to put the young guests during the courses, seminars and festivals. The huge unused loft spaces were an obvious choice, so they were restored, insulated and provided with roof windows.

The ancient castle is very much a vibrant part of Europe today. And in the castle and the park, with an oak tree more than a thousand years old, young guests find friends, inspiration and fantasies for tomorrow.

Château de Brie-Comte-Robert is a square, low-walled structure with round corner towers, a very typical example of many of France's medieval castles. A large part of the castle wall has been rebuilt, along with all eight of its towers.

Friends of an old castle: Château de Brie-Comte-Robert, Seine-et-Marne, France

One example of the many heritage sites scattered across Europe, unknown to most people except the locals, is the Château de Brie-Comte-Robert south east of Paris, in the hilly landscape of Brie. Few know of the castle – even guidebooks mention it only in passing.

According to historians, this castle is a very typical example of many of France's medieval castles. The Château de Brie-Comte-Robert is a square, low-walled structure with round corner towers, just a few steps away from the market square in the centre of the small town bearing the same name.

The castle was built in medieval times in the late 1100s by a brother of the French King Louis VII, Robert de Dreux, who was Lord of Brie among many other possessions. This was the age of knights and damsels, of crusades, wars and feuding. The perpetual unrest was the reason for the construction of strong fortress walls, moats and defence turrets. The lords and seigneurs owned many different castles and homes in their often widespread lands and properties. The lord and his numerous entourage, including armed men, moved from one place to another during the year in order to collect and consume the substantial taxes paid by his

peasants in the form of products like grain, meat, wine, vegetables, beer, cheese, cloth and coal.

A couple of centuries later, in the 1500s, the castle was mainly deserted and fell into disrepair as more peaceful times dawned. During the coming centuries a succession of noble or royal owners repaired the castle, pulled down towers and demolished the upper part of the walls, which were no longer needed, or erected new buildings. And as final decline set in, even the courtyard was filled in with soil to serve as a vegetable garden.

In 1982, there came a radical change in the long history of the almost-obliterated castle: the 'Amis du Vieux Château', an association of voluntary workers interested in historic heritage, began reconstructing the thick limestone walls. Since then, a large part of the castle wall has been rebuilt, along with all eight of its towers. No mean feat! Excavations in the inner courtyard have turned up numerous wall fragments and objects from former living quarters. The voluntary excavators have been supported by a large number of private and public sponsors, who also provided the financial basis for the Friends of the Old Castle to undertake their most ambitious project yet in 2003: the building of a combined administration and exhibition building, or, in official French, a CIP, Centre d'Interprétation du Patrimoine.

The national authority for the preservation of historic monuments (ACMH) recommended a timber structure – partly because this material would differ clearly from the old walls and partly because a wooden structure could be taken down again relatively easily to accommodate later, more extensive excavations.

Thanks to the efforts of the members of the Amis du Vieux Château, the castle today functions as an exhibition hall and educational centre.

The all-pervading, ever-changing daylight coming through the roof windows illuminates the historic artefacts, the reconstructed masonry and the new, lightweight wooden construction.

The Parisian Eric Colmet Daâge succeeded in convincing the owner to sell the Captain's ancient stone house from 1780 on the Île de Batz.

The room is covered with oak panelling like the original panelling from the eighteenth century. Eric Colmet Daâge has a passion for antiques as well as for houses. He enjoys the process of restoring in his workroom.

The house-lover: Île de Batz, Finistère, Brittany, France

"When I was a child, my parents took me here to Île de Batz on picnics. Later, I brought my own son and daughter, and it was during one of those trips that I fell in love with this old deserted stone house," Eric Colmet Daâge says. "I very much enjoy restoring old houses, getting them as close as possible to their original state. This place is magical, and the view from here is fantastic. At that time you could get into the garden even when the house was locked up. Practically all the houses here on the island are still owned by farmers and fishermen, but I really wanted it so much, and with a lot of work and persuasion I succeeded in buying it without ever having seen it from the inside."

The Île de Batz, off the coast at the town of Roscoff at the tip of Brittany, really is 'the end of the world', which is what the name of the region, Finistère, means. This is where France ends and the Atlantic takes over. An atmosphere of bygone times can be felt everywhere among the traditional stone houses with black slate roofs. Horses are used in the fields, and since few cars are allowed, transport is mainly by small tractors. The islanders do not want their little corner of Paradise to be turned into second homes for Parisians, so they very seldom sell to outsiders. Despite

An atmosphere of bygone times can be felt everywhere among the traditional stone houses with black slate roofs.

When Eric Colmet Daâge was a child, his parents took him to the Île de Batz on picnics. Later, he brought his own son and daughter and it was during one of these trips that he fell in love with the old deserted stone house.

The Île de Batz, off the coast at the town of Roscoff at the tip of Brittany, really is 'the end of the world', which is what the name of the region, Finistère, means.

this, the Parisian Eric Colmet Daâge succeeded in convincing the owner to sell the ancient 'Captain's stone house' from 1780.

"I was very excited when I entered the house for the first time. It was a real gem! But a gem in decay, as the roof had leaked for several years, so all the wooden structures in the house had rotted and had to be replaced: the roof construction, the supporting floor beams, the floors. Luckily the huge stone chimneypieces were intact.

"I decided to try re-creating the house as closely as possible to the way it would have been in 1780. I am passionate about the house, and it really deserves to be restored."

For the Captain's House on the Île de Batz he imported 80 tonnes of granite to recreate the original granite floors. The beautiful solid oak staircase from the eighteenth century was bought in Paris and transported to the island; and the entire interior of the house is to be covered with copies of the original oak panelling.

"The only departure from the eighteenth century is the roof windows in the attic. Luckily I found a very small model, so they're discreet. And here in Brittany, VELUX is such an integral part of the Breton architecture that it would almost be an aberration if there weren't any!

I've been working on this house for ten years, but it isn't finished yet. We only spent a night here for the first time last summer when we held an exhibition of Lartigue photos from the old Île de Batz in the house." Eric is the editor of the magazine Photo and enjoyed combining his two passions, houses and photos, there.

"I love scouting for antiques to put in my houses, restoring them in my workroom. I look forward to coming here every time! Just as I look forward to my other houses in Porquerolles and in the Alps, which also need a caring hand."

As great industries of the north closed down, the Victorian estate fell into dilapidation and desolation.

The characteristic profile of the Victorian estate's chimneys has been re-interpreted in the reconstruction process.

The architects have moved the downstairs up and the upstairs down, creating a bright living room upstairs which opens to new pedestrian paths, courtyards and gardens placed on the new garage roofs.

From smoke to daylight: Chimney Pot Park, Salford, Manchester, England

Victorian housing in industrial areas of England traditionally consisted of small terraced houses often nicknamed 'two-up, two-down' or 'back-to-back'. The houses would typically have a kitchen and a living room downstairs and two bedrooms upstairs, with a huge chimney in each house gathering together the chimney pipes from the open fireplaces of each room. The front of the house would face the street, and the back would open up to an enclosed yard with a narrow back alley in between the houses. During the 1800s housing estates like this were built in large numbers in British towns and cities as housing for the huge population of workers in the new prosperous industries. Such space allotted to a family, and the high standard of these workers' homes, were regarded as new ideals and copied in several other European countries.

Seedley and Langworthy in Salford near Manchester are two such estates of 349 Victorian terraced houses. Like so many similar estates, they lost out as the great industries of the north closed down and the area changed. Nobody really wanted to live there any more. Neglect and long-term underinvestment as well as growing crime all created a vicious circle, making it a place re-

The chimney pots were to be the focal point of the reborn estate. The walls at the front of the building were kept – everything else had to be built up. The chimney pots were made into light shafts instead of chimneys, and in a unique way the VELUX windows were installed on top of pre-made shafts resembling traditional chimneys.

jected rather than a place of choice.

What was to be done about such a heritage? The houses were practically worthless and largely uninhabited. Several streets were bought up wholesale so the houses could be completely demolished to make room for the construction of new contemporary housing. But the local heritage council insisted that the distinctive chimneys so typical of the houses should be preserved, as should the Victorian layout of the area and the brick façades.

A group of architects, Urban Splash, came up with some unusual ideas. If the chimneys had to be preserved as a landmark, why not use them for a completely different purpose: letting daylight into the houses instead of smoke out of the houses? Why not turn the houses upside down, using the light? VELUX was engaged to deliver a solution for the chimney/light well that made the amazing transformation possible.

The two estates were completely reconstructed and rebuilt behind the old brick façades: the back yards and narrow alleyways were covered over. Parking spaces for the future owners were created in the lower part, and on top new raised-level garden/patios were built: private spaces with footpaths. The living room/kitchen floor was placed on the first floor, with large windows opening out to the new gardens. Bedrooms were placed on the ground floor. The top floor under the sloping roof was given an extra mezzanine with light coming in from the chimney light shaft.

Advance interest in acquiring a home in the transformed 'Chimney Pot Park' was huge. A special favourable price to first-time homebuyers made it possible for young people to get a first home at an affordable price.

Today Chimney Pot Park is a living part of the new revival of the north. Gone are the old, dirty industries; instead, the Manchester area of today is a centre of industry in a new age with its eyes on the future – but with its heritage from the industrial age well-preserved amidst contemporary life.

In the reborn Chimney Pot Park, the former back alleys have been covered and serve as garages beneath new green gardens.

Facelift and Botox
for an ageing beauty:
Brno, Czech Republic

During the Communist era, the elegant house in Brno served as a state health care institution. The façade was painted in the official socialist green colour, the magnificent interior was destroyed, and new ugly houses crowded in on both sides.

An elegant house in the Czech city of Brno stands out from other houses in the street with its richly structured façade and imposing proportions. The house is registered on the Czech National Architectural Heritage List as an example of neo-Renaissance architecture inspired by the Northern and French Renaissance. But its good looks are a recent phenomenon, as this is a resurrected beauty that lay dormant for half a century.

Originally the mansion was built as a private family residence of a prominent, wealthy local factory-owner around the end of the nineteenth century. This was the heyday of the Austro-Hungarian Empire, when Brno was the leading centre of the new industrial age in the province of Moravia.

After the Second World War, the new Communist regime of Czechoslovakia confiscated the house from its original owner and it lost all traces of its former beauty. It became a state-administered property and underwent the less-than-tender mercies of being remodelled as a Socialist health care institution. The façade was painted in the official socialist green colour, the magnificent interior was destroyed, and new ugly houses crowded in on both sides.

The villa is registered on the Czech National Architectural Heritage List as an example of neo-Renaissance architecture inspired by the Northern and French Renaissance. Its good looks are a recent phenomenon, since this is a resurrected beauty that lay dormant for half a century.

But the country underwent drastic changes: the Communist regime in Czechoslovakia fell in 1989, and a few years later the country was divided peacefully into two independent states: the Czech Republic and Slovakia. The house slept on, ugly and dilapidated, and it was not until 1999 that it was given the kiss of life. Once again a private property, it was more than ready to be brought back to its former splendour, so a restoration process took place in 2003-04.

New features and contemporary structural solutions were necessary to restore the house in its former beauty, and the project was undertaken in full compliance with the requirements of the Brno City Council's Department for the Preservation of Historic Monuments and the National Institute for the Preservation of Historic Monuments in Brno. The architects discovered that the foundations and the supporting walls were damp right up to the level of the first floor. The reason was that the foundations of the cellars were much older than the house itself, and even turned out to be linked with a system of cellars that once connected the original buildings with a nearby Gothic monastery!

The plan for the restoration was to maximise the amount of living space, to make the entire house lighter and open it up towards the gardens, and to enhance its unique historical value. The reception area on the ground floor was made into offices, while two apartments were created on the second floor and on the loft floor with the charming turrets; and indeed two delightful apartments permeated by daylight from roof windows were created. In the rooms without direct access to natural light, sun tunnels were installed. The windows were placed to offer intriguing views towards the roof turrets and the garden.

Once again this ageing beauty can be enjoyed thanks to the delicate skills of the beauty specialists!

Once again this ageing beauty can be enjoyed because of the delicate skills of the beauty specialists!

278

Creating
future visions
for daylight

Creating future visions for daylight

Mr Villum Kann Rasmussen, the inventor of the VELUX roof window, was foresighted in his perception of the needs of customers. Before most others, he understood the new dream images of family life and their consequences for the home. By letting daylight in through roof windows, people could change unused, undesirable loft space into much-desired bright children's rooms, bedrooms and bathrooms.

In a new millennium, new generations are again creating their homes. They too have new dream images of how a good life should be and what a home should be like. Their dream images challenge their present home environments. They want more daylight everywhere in their homes - even in the wardrobe - and they want to erase the boundaries between outside and inside. But concerned about more than the purely aesthetic aspects of their homes, they also nurture dreams of creating a better future world for their children by contributing to a sustainable environment and by reducing emissions of destructive CO_2 into the atmosphere.

True to the focus on the importance and the power of daylight, and to the founder's tradition of foresightedness, VELUX is developing new perspectives and products to enable customers to fulfil these new dreams of the future in their everyday life.

Energy produced by daylight: the power of the sun
What if one consequence of living in daylight was that a home would use no fossil fuel at all, and thus emit no CO_2? What if a home could even produce energy and actively contribute to a better environment? What if a home could help to improve the health of people living there?

These are the challenges VELUX has taken up in the new millennium by engaging in research and experiments in cooperation with others from the fields of solar energy, photovoltaics, solar-heating systems and architecture, to work towards common goals for the future. These visions are now taking physical shape in the design and construction of model homes.

The future is active
Until now, most attempts to reduce CO_2 emission from homes

have involved building houses where insulation ensured that heat did not escape easily and thus that the consumption of fossil fuel was reduced.

The latest generation of inventive houses being developed may be called 'active houses' because they actively use the power of daylight to produce energy for lighting, heating and ventilation and even to produce electricity for household appliances. These new active houses will give a whole new meaning to the concept of living in daylight!

Mr Villum Kann Rasmussen believed in the principle that an experiment is better than a thousand expert opinions. True to this belief, VELUX is experimenting with models for the homes of the future in the project 'Model Home 2020'.
The principle behind Model Home 2020 is the conviction that in order to create a sustainable future, it is essential to see a house as a total entity, considering not only its energy consumption but its total emission of CO_2. If CO_2 emissions can be reduced through the use of sustainable energy produced by the house with daylight as the energy source, the occupants of the house will be able to use energy as they wish while living in a healthy and comfortable home.

Model Home 2020 will bring a whole new future meaning to the concept of living in daylight.

Lumina House, Wrocław, Poland

Lumina House, designed by Archipelag, is saturated with daylight thanks to the use of a much larger roof-window area than is usual in traditional houses. The need for electric light is minimal during daytime, even in the innermost corners of the house. The feeling of being outdoors while indoors is ensured in the living-room areas - and surprisingly also in the bedroom and bathroom areas - by the inventive use of roof windows. Lumina House has a healthily ventilated indoor climate all year round. Solar panels are the main contributor to the heating of the water for the household.

Why pay for artificial light when you can get daylight for free? To achieve many different 'light zones', Lumina House has a combination of various levels and directions of daylight intake, so each part of the home gets its own character, view, lighting and materials.

The main bedroom has plenty of daylight coming through windows placed one above the other, and this brings the light deep into the room and blurs the borderline between outdoors and indoors.

The walk-in closet has natural daylight from two sun tunnels in the ceiling.

Why pay for artificial light, when you can get daylight for free? To achieve many different 'light zones', Lumina house has a combination of various levels and directions of daylight intake so each part of the home gets its own character, view, lighting and materials.

SOLTAG is placed on top of an existing flat-roofed building in need of renovation. Daylight produces the necessary heating through solar panels. The sloping surface of the roof lets in twice as much light as a horizontal one.

SOLTAG, Hørsholm, Denmark

By positioning the house with the majority of its roof windows, all solar panels and photovoltaics facing south, the solar heat intake and daylight conditions are optimised. Heating insulation and ventilation have both been considered in creating this sustainable house aiming at balancing energy absorption, insulation capacity and air exchange.

A great challenge of the future is the problem of what to do about the huge mass of housing constructed in Europe in the 1960s and 1970s with poor insulation, causing considerable energy waste and CO_2 emissions. In general the period favoured flat roofs, which are now often in dire need of renovation. One possible solution is to add the SOLTAG (i.e. sun-roof) house to the top of the existing building as a completely new top floor. This gives the building much-needed insulation, a new roof, and as an added bonus it is self-sufficient in terms of energy, since it provides CO_2-neutral heating with solar energy.

The SOLTAG is placed on top of an existing flat-roofed building in need of renovation. Daylight produces the necessary heating through solar panels. The sloping surface of the roof lets in twice as much light as a horizontal one.

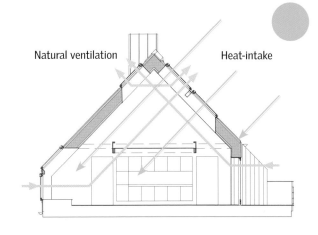

Natural ventilation   Heat-intake

Home for Life produces its own energy from daylight and even sends surplus energy back into the electricity grid.

Glass panels in the living room of Home for Life enhance and distribute the daylight effect from the roof windows.

Home for Life, Lystrup, Århus, Denmark, 2009

The objective of the Home for Life project is to design and construct a house that produces more energy than is consumed by its occupants, and to make all this energy sustainable. Solar collectors will produce hot water, and heat pumps will convert heat from the air into heating for the rooms as well as supplement the hot water. Photovoltaic solar panels integrated in the south-sloping roof will produce the electricity necessary to power this system as well as electricity for household purposes.

Home for Life produces its own energy from daylight and even sends surplus energy back into the electricity grid.

The Home for Life house is made for comfortable living and for contact between outdoors and indoors. A large, glazed veranda can be opened up completely in summertime, while it can be closed off and function as a glass conservatory for plants and flowers during the colder times of the year. The window area is considerably larger than in a traditional house, especially the roof-window area.

Glass panels in the living room of the Home for Life house enhance and distribute the daylight effect from the roof windows.

288

Solar-Aktivhaus, Austria, 2009

The rather traditional look of the Austrian 'Solar-Active' house is deceptive, since it is definitely no ordinary house! At least not at present - but perhaps it will be in the future. The house produces its own warm water, its own heat and its own electricity. Additionally it could produce its own coolness during the summer. The house offers the best indoor climate throughout the year thanks to a controlled air exchange. Even during the cold Austrian winter, the house is producing its own heat and does not need any energy from the outside. The house regulates its temperature automatically and individually in each room and also automatically assures a healthy ventilation by circulation of fresh air. Sometimes the house even produces electricity for the public electricity grid.

The house is much more open to the outside than a traditional house: this gives more natural light during the dark winter days to the residents. And also reduces the electricity consumption for light.

In this house, the most recent technology is used and the design is able to incorporate future technologies like producing electricity from thermal solar collectors.

The Solar-Active house is saturated with daylight - also from roof windows. The more sky you can see from the room, the more daylight you will get. It produces more energy than it consumes, contributing to a sustainable future.

The Solar-Active house is saturated by daylight also from roof windows. The more sky you can see from the room, the more daylight you will get. It produces more energy than it consumes, contributing to a sustainable future.

Zero-Carbon Town House, Breidablick, Roskilde, Denmark, 2009

Most Europeans today live in towns and cities, and in the future their number will only grow. These European town-dwellers also dream of a home that contributes to sustainable energy, that is filled with daylight and that permits contact between the inside and the outside. That is a challenge for the future!

A Danish project has designed a model house for town living which will meet all these wishes: the Zero-Carbon Town House, a home constructed on the principle of 'active-house energy'. The town house takes its inspiration from two ancient energy-efficient models: the low English terraced houses and the Roman atrium house with an inner courtyard. The open atrium space in the middle of the Zero-Carbon House does not open up freely to the sky like its Roman inspiration, but is covered by roof windows that admit daylight in a similar way, giving the occupants the feeling of living in daylight.

People living in the Zero-Carbon Town House will be able to contribute to a sustainable future by using the power of daylight, since solar panels will supply hot domestic water and warm air for the heating systems, while solar cells will produce electricity for household appliances and send surplus back into the local electricity grid.

The Zero-Carbon Town House offers city- and town-dwelling Europeans the opportunity to live in daylight, while contributing actively to a better environment in the future.

The Zero-Carbon Town House offers a possibility to Europeans living in cities and towns of living in daylight while contributing actively to a better environment in the future.

Things you did not know

The name VELUX derives from VE for ventilation and LUX, the Latin word for light – the two primary elements in Villum Kann Rasmussen's development of the VELUX roof window.

In several countries in the world, VELUX is a brand better known than many soft drinks and cars – quite extraordinary for a building component.

Before the VELUX roof window was developed, the loft was primarily used for storing purposes or for house servants, poor poets, painters and students. In some towns even as a stable for cows.

The first VELUX roof windows were installed in the primary school Slagelse Vestre Skole in 1942, the same year VELUX was registered as a trademark. Today there are approximately 42 million inhabited attics in Europe.

About every third European believes the best place in the house is the room under the sloping roof.

It is often much cheaper to build an extra storey or to utilise the attic than to build a house extension.

VELUX roof windows are installed in homes from the North of Greenland to the Australian outback and in buildings from the Louvre in Paris to Beijing University in China.

Several millions of people sleep under a VELUX roof window every night.

A VELUX roof window gives up to 40% more daylight in the room than a dormer.

40% of the world's total energy consumption is used for heating, cooling and electricity in buildings. To build a sustainable future, the amount of energy used in buildings and CO_2 emitted from buildings must be reduced. Daylight, heat gain from the sun and natural ventilation are part of the solution.

Working in daylight environments results in higher productivity (Visher 1989).

Learning in daylit environments results in more effective learning – up to 20% improvement has been seen in tests in California (Heschong et al. 1999).

Villum Kann Rasmussen placed great importance on the ability to condition daylight. The first blinds for VELUX roof windows were produced in 1973.

Today, a large variety of blinds are available for VELUX roof windows and the amount of fabric used for manufacturing VELUX blinds can cover the distance between Hamburg and Paris.

Human beings spend 90% of their time indoors; consequently, daylight and fresh air in buildings are of vital importance.

An average person eats 2 kg of food per day. On average we consume 15 kg of air per day by breathing; consequently, the quality of the air we breathe is of great importance.

The available solar energy exceeds the world's energy consumption by a factor of 1,500 (R. Perez et al.).

The solar energy contribution to buildings through VELUX roof windows in Europe is estimated to be similar to the energy generated by just over three average-sized power plants.

Special thanks

This journey of exploration through the countries of Europe in search of homes and workplaces where people enjoy living in daylight has been an extraordinary endeavour. The book would never have been created without cooperation, help, assistance, enthusiasm, openness, willingness, patience and enduring belief in its purpose from so many different people.

My very warm thanks to all the many people who have willingly opened their homes and workplaces, showing how they enjoy living in daylight. And a thank-you to the VELUX employees from all over Europe who have patiently listened to the ideas and concepts of the book and supplied practical contacts and assistance, without which this book would never have been possible.

Special thanks to Inge Mette Pretzmann from VELUX for enabling and maintaining the contacts to local VELUX offices around Europe, for explaining the purpose of the book and for getting all the necessary information back to me; for an enthusiastic sparring partnership and for even participating in interviews.

To Nina Matthiesen, who organised the innumerable items of information and photos; and made sure we never lost the thread. To historian Steen Schøn who opened up a treasure-chest of old photos from the archives. And to my husband, Niels Holm Svendsen, for professional editorial advice and for happily enduring eight months of perspectives on life seen mainly through roof windows.

Thanks to the many photographers who have helped to give the book its important visual dimension – both the many professional photographers and the enthusiastic amateur photographers from flickr.com.

Thank you to Lars E. Kann-Rasmussen for an inspired, engaged and positive dialogue all through the creation process. You changed my way of looking at European architecture!

Copenhagen, October 1st 2008

Maria-Therese Hoppe
mthoppe@gmail.com

Architects and photographers

FRONT PAGE, PHOTOGRA-
PHY: Kenneth Havgaard
Flyleaf photo: Torben Eskerod
Photo page 4: Torben Eskerod
Back cover photos: M. Jurcovic
Photos page 6, 8: VKR
Holding, History & Library
Services

LIVING IN DAYLIGHT,
INTRODUCTION
Photo page 10: Pegaz/
Alamy, Imageselect
Photo page 13: Glen Allison,
Getty Images
Photo page 14: Vincent
Ricardel, Getty Images
Photo page 15: Giant
Ginkgo's, Flickr
Photo page 16: Ugyen
Namgyel
Photos page 17, 18, 19, 20,
21, 22, 23, 24, 25: VKR
Holding, History & Library
Services
Photos page 22, 25 bottom:
VELUX own photos
Page 18: Drawing by Müller
Kully

CHANGING THE HOME
AN ILLUMINATED DARK-
ROOM, AMSTERDAM,
NETHERLANDS
Photos: Torben Eskerod
Photo page 30: Elisabeth
Merle Petersen
Attic architecture and
interior design: Elisabeth
Merle Petersen

COUNTRYSIDE VIEWS,
BARNFIELDS, STAFFORD-
SHIRE MOORLANDS,
ENGLAND
Photos of house: Jeremy
Phillips
Staffordshire moorlands:
John G. Morris
Architect: Associated

Architects LLP
www.associated-architects.
co.uk

LIVING IN A COWHOUSE,
ERFTSTADT, RHEIN-
ERFTKREIS, GERMANY
Photos: Stefan Sonn
Idea and architecture by
Herbert Adler

A MINISTER AT HOME:
TALLIN, NOMME, ESTONIA
Photos of house: Kiristjan
Lepp, 'Kroonika'
Tallin: ©AllOver Photography/
Alamy
Architect: Architecture
Studio Kirsima & Niineväli

BUILDING BLOCKS OF
LIGHT AND SHADE:
HØRSHOLM, DENMARK
Interior photos: Kenneth
Havgaard
Photo of construction:
Thomas Kent Larsen
Architect: Werner Thomas
Mathies

A BARN FOR THREE
GENERATIONS, BUCHS,
ZÜRICH, SWITZERLAND
Photos: Ruedi Walti
Architect: werk1 architeken
und planer ag

PARENTS' DELIGHT, PARIS,
FRANCE
Photos: Torben Eskerod

TEENAGERS IN THE HOUSE,
LAKE BLED, SLOVENIA
Photos: Lake Bled: Steve
Rollins
Photos of house: Tomaz
Bercic

KITCHEN GARAGE,
BIRKERØD, DENMARK
Photos: Jacob Boserup
Architect: Lena and Michael
Hoff

SIAMESE TWINS: ZAGREB,
CROATIA
Photos: Sandro Lendler
Photo before renovation:
Miloš Pecotic
Architect: Miloš Pecotic

A BATHROOM WITH A
VIEW, LE CONQUET,
FRANCE
Photos: Torben Eskerod
Photo page 82: Glyn
Orpwood

BACK TO THE FUTURE,
AARHUS, DENMARK
Photo: Barslund + Kaslov
Architect: Mads Riis

BACK TO THE VILLAGE IN
LUXURY, QUINTA DE
ALDEIA, AVANCA, PORTU-
GAL
Photos: Torben Eskerod
Architect: Maria Teresa
Almendra

CHOOSING THE HOME
Photo page 94: Adam Mørk

NORTHERN LIGHTS AND
SEA VIEWS, NÆRØY,
NORWAY
Photos: Adam Mørk
Architecture: Mesterhus-
Norge

MOUNTAIN RETREAT, DAS,
SPAIN
Photos: Eugeni Pons
Architect: Carles Gelpí

BACK TO BACK, HELSING-
BORG, SWEDEN

Photos: Ole Ziegler

CHILD'S PLAY, HAGENEI-
LAND, YPENBURG, NETHER-
LANDS
Photos: Adam Mørk, Torben
Eskerod
Architect: MVRDV

INTELLIGENT LUXURY IN
THE DATCHA, KOROVINO,
KRASNOGORSKY, MOSCOW,
RUSSIA
Photos: Vladimir Timchuk
Photo of Arkhangelskoe
Palace: Vladphotos/Alamy

COUNTRY LIVING IN A
MEGALOPOLIS, CEKMEKÖY,
ISTANBUL, TURKEY
Photos: Uluç Őzcű

CHOOSING CITY LIFE,
ARMADA, S'HERTOGEN-
BOSCH, NETHERLANDS
Photos: Torben Eskerod
Architect: Tony McGuirk,
Building Design Partnership
(BDP)

LIGHTING UP THE CITY
LOFT
Photo page 132: Àngel Luis
Baltanás Ramirez
Photo page 134: The Royal
Library, Copenhagen.
Painting page 134: The poor
poet by German artist Carl
Spitzweg
Photo page 137: The Museum
of Copenhagen

SPACE AND LIGHT IN A
CITY LOFT, MADRID, SPAIN
Photos: Àngel Luis Baltanás
Ramirez
Architects: Juan Carnicero
García and Gálata Sáenz
Mariscal, Gálata+Juan

HERITAGE CHALLENGES,
BUDAPEST, HUNGARY
Photo interior: Edina Ligeti,
Photo exterior: Gábor Fényes
Architect: Lázló Benczúr jr.

THE HEAVY BURDEN OF
HISTORY, NIPPES, COLOGNE,
GERMANY
Photos: Constantin Meyer
Architect: Luczak Architekten

GREEN OASIS IN THE CITY
OF FASHION, MILAN, ITALY
Architect: Francesco Florulli
Milan photo: Daniel Schwabe
Photo of house: VELUX Italy
Photographer unknown

SELF-MADE IS WELL-
MADE, AMAGER, DENMARK
Photos: Tariq Mikkel Khan/
Polfoto
Photo from Amager
Strandpark: Torben Eskerod
Architect: Klaus Malmgren

RAISING THE ROOF, ST.
PETERSBURG, RUSSIA
Photos: Torben Eskerod

A CLEAN ENVIRONMENT
AND RECYCLING, VIENNA,
AUSTRIA
Photos: Adam Mørk
Old photos: photographer
unknown
Architect: Armin Mohsen
Daneshgar, Daneshgar
Architects

STAYING AT HOME,
BUCHAREST, ROMANIA
Photo of glass covered
Bucharest street: Nicoleta
Apostol
Photo of old building façade:
Corneliu Munteanu
Interior photos: Torben
Eskerod

Architect: Madalina Petrescu

AN ARTIST'S STUDIO,
PARIS, FRANCE
Drawing: Florine Asch
Paris photos: Torben Eskerod
Interior photos: Guillaume de
Laubier

STUDIO INHERITANCE,
SOFIA, BULGARIA
Photos of building: Ruslan
Popov
Photo of city: Caro/Alamy
Architects: Bozhidar Hinkov
and Daniela Slavova

WORKING UNDER THE
ROOF
Photo page 182: Torben
Eskerod
Photos page 184: The
Museum of Copenhagen
Photo page 186: Till Krech
Office cubes page 187: John
T. Nguyen
Office workers page 187:
ACE Stock

JUGEND MALLS, BERLIN,
GERMANY
Photos: Stefan Müller
Architect: A+O Berlin
Architektur + Organisation,
Freie Architekten + Berater,
Frank Hüpperling, Stephan
Vieweger
Denkmalpflegerische
Begleitung: Hübner + Oehmig
Büro für Architektur und
Denkmalpflege

IT AND DEMOCRACY,
ASSEMBLEIA DA REPÚ-
BLICA, LISBON, PORTUGAL
Photos: Torben Eskerod

MUSIC IN THE DOCKS,
COPENHAGEN, DENMARK
Photo page 196: Adam Mørk
Photo page 197: Torben
Eskerod
Photo page 198: Ole

Christiansen
Concert photo page 199: Ole
Christiansen
Interior photo page 199:
Adam Mørk
Architect: Frank Maali

RAILWAY ROMANCE:
LAUSANNE, SWITZERLAND
Photo of Flon: Antoine
Rouleau
Photo of Gymnase du
Bugnon: Thomas Jantscher
Photo page 204: Michel
Fillian
Architect: CCHE Architecture
SIA, Lausanne

WAR AND PEACE, SARAJE-
VO, BOSNIA-HERZEGOVINA
Photos: VELUX

A CHOCOLATE JUNGLE IN
THE HAYLOFT, ØRSHOLT,
DENMARK
Photos: Torben Eskerod
Architecture of renovation:
Peter Beier

FROM GUNPOWDER TO
WEB SHOP, KRISTIANSAND,
NORWAY
Photos: Ole Ziegler
Photo page 213: Marit
Simonstad Kraale

GIANT ROOFS: GDAŃSK,
POLAND
Photos of university interiors:
Torben Eskerod
Photo page 219: photogra-
pher unknown
Photo of Gdańsk street page
220: Miles Ertman
Architecture of renovation:
architect Wieslaw Czabanski

PRESERVING HISTORIC
HERITAGE
Photo page 224: Torben
Eskerod

CENTURIES OF HEALTH
CARE, HÔTEL DIEU, PARIS,
FRANCE
Photo: Torben Eskerod
Architect: Alain-Charles
Perrot, architect of historic
monuments.

CENTURIES OF POWER,
PALAIS DE JUSTICE, PARIS,
FRANCE
Photo: Torben Eskerod
Architect: Alain-Charles
Perrot, architect of historical
monuments.

CENTURIES OF FUN,
PALAIS ROYAL, PARIS,
FRANCE
Photos: Torben Eskerod
©Daniel Buren/billedkunst.dk
Daniel Buren »Souvenir: Les
Deux Plateaux«, sculptures
displayed, in the main
courtyard of Palais Royal
gardens, Paris 1985-1986

GAMBLING, SHOOTING,
SWIMMING AND DRINKING,
PESTSZENTLÖRINC,
HUNGARY
Photos: Gábor Fényes
Historical photo - unknown
Architect: Molnár és Port

A BALTIC JEWEL SET IN
GOLD: ST PETERSBURG,
RUSSIA
Photos: Torben Eskerod

HIPPIE NOSTALGIA,
COPENHAGEN, DENMARK
Photo: Torben Eskerod
Air-photo of ravelin and
Christiania and Copenhagen:
©Philip Menke
Photo page 250, top: Anne P.
Schaldemose

KNIGHTS' TALES AND
STORYTELLERS: LIMBURG,
BELGIUM
Photo page 252: Knightwise,

Belgium; www.knightwise.
com
Photo page 253-255: The
Landcommandery, Alden
Biesen

FRIENDS OF AN OLD
CASTLE: CHÂTEAU DE
BRIE-COMTE-ROBERT,
FRANCE
Photos: Adam Mørk
Architect: SCP Semon
Rapaport
Exhibition design: Lorenzo
Piqueras
Academic concept and
archaeological research: Amis
du Vieux Château, Brie-
Comte-Robert.

THE HOUSE-LOVER: ÎLE DE
BATZ, FRANCE
Photos: Torben Eskerod
Renovation architecture: Eric
Colmet Daâge

FROM SMOKE TO DAY-
LIGHT, SALFORD, ENGLAND
Page 273: computer
generated image from
©Uniform
Photos: Torben Eskerod
Photo before renovation:
Peter Alkjær
Architecture: Urban Splash

FACELIFT AND BOTOX FOR
AN AGEING BEAUTY, BRNO,
CZECH REPUBLIC
Architecture: Vlasta Loutocká
and Zdenka Softicová, Form
Arch
Photos before renovation:
Ing. Arch. Vlasta Loutocka
Photos after renovation:
VELUX photos, photographer
unknown

CREATING FUTURE VISIONS
FOR DAYLIGHT
Lumina House, Wrocław,
Poland:
Architecture: Artur Wóciak,

Archipelag.
Computer generated images:
Archipelag and VELUX

SOLTAG, HØRSHOLM,
DENMARK
www.soltag.net
Photo: Adam Mørk
Rendering: Marcel Schwarz,
Rubow architects
Architecture: Rubow &
Nielsen Architects

HOME FOR LIFE, LYSTRUP,
DENMARK
Renderings and Architecture:
Aart A/S

SOLAR-AKTIV HAUS,
AUSTRIA
Architecture: Georg W.
Reinberg, www.reinberg.net
Rendering: Architekturbuero
Reinberg ZT GmbH

ZERO-CARBON TOWN-
HOUSE, ROSKILDE,
DENMARK
The Breidablick project
Architecture: Rubow
architects
Rendering: Marcel Schwarz,
Rubow architects

For all photos we have tried
to find the photographer as
well as identifiy the persons
on the photos, in order to
credit them and obtain
permission. Unfortunately,
this has not been possible in
all cases. Likewise, it has not
been possible to identify the
architect of all projects.